Hope Alive
GOING AND GROWING
THROUGH PAIN

By
Matthew R. S. Todd

Mill Lake Books

Published by Mill Lake Books
Abbotsford, BC
Canada

Printed by Lightning Source, distributed by Ingram

Cover design by Dean Tjepkema

Scripture verses marked NIV are taken from THE HOLY BIBLE,
NEW INTERNATIONAL VERSION®, NIV® Copyright © 1973,
1978, 1984, 2011 by Biblica, Inc.® Used by permission. All
rights reserved worldwide.

Scripture verses marked NASB are taken from the NEW
AMERICAN STANDARD BIBLE®, Copyright ©
1960,1962,1963,1968,1971,1972,1973,1975,1977,1995 by
The Lockman Foundation. Used by permission.

Scripture verses marked The Message are taken from *The
Message*. Copyright © 1993, 1994, 1995, 1996, 2000, 2001,
2002. Used by permission of NavPress Publishing Group.

ISBN 978-0-9951983-0-2

Endorsements

Matthew Todd has compiled an impressive group of personal narratives built around his life as a husband, a father, a pastor, and a professional. He uses these to reflect on the problem of evil in human life, but he offers no simple answer apart from the comforting thought that God is always with us no matter what we face. The encounter with God is typically at the points in life where we are stretched almost beyond our limits—in personal experience. Matthew demonstrates this admirably in his book.

Phillip H. Wiebe, PhD
Professor of Philosophy
Chair of Research Ethics Board
Trinity Western University, Canada
Vancouver Shroud Association Director

If I want transparent and informed friends to help me grasp unfathomable and unanswerable suffering, I want Matthew Todd to be in that conversation. This book combines realistic and hopeful perspectives, not only drawing from the narrative of his life but also utilizing the thoughtful and even artful contributions of global thinkers. Together, these perspectives bring hope and the encouragement to find joy.

Randy White, DMin
Director, Fresno Pacific University
Center for Community Transformation,
and author of Poetic Intercessions:
Artful Prayers for a Friend
(*Harmon Press, 2010)*

Dedication

"When Jesus saw her weeping, and the Jews who had come along with her also weeping, he was deeply moved in spirit and troubled." – John 11:33 NIV

"Jesus wept." – John 11:35 NIV

At the time of writing this volume, a good friend of mine is suffering with an incurable brain disease and had his house burn down. On the global front, the Western world is witnessing one of the largest refugee crises since the Second World War, coming out of Syria. These circumstances represent different dimensions of the suffering that is discussed in these chapters.

This book is dedicated to Sheldon, my family, my friends, and my social network connections, who, like all thinking human beings, have struggled to grasp why God allows pain and struggles to befall people, including those who love God. Suffering has the ability to stop people in their tracks and force them to wrestle with mortality and life's deeper spiritual questions. This is what happened with my maternal grandparents after my grandmother had a debilitating stroke. A Christian neighbor, who brought my grandmother swimming and to church services, reintroduced them to the resources of faith and Christian community. My prayer is that this volume may help you to simply trust that God is always good, even though some of what He allows can leave us speechless. May you find here Good News, encouragement, and hope.

Contents

Introduction: Theodicy and Godspell 9

1. Hope Alive: Knock, Knock, Knocking on Heaven's Door 13

2. Hope Alive: Humpty Dumpty Had a Great Fall . 21

3. Hope Alive: After the Pink Slip 33

4. Hope Alive: The Big Bang Theory 39

5. Hope Alive: It Comes in Threes........................... 43

6. Hope Alive: It's Murder 49

7. Hope Alive: This Is Mental................................ 55

8. Hope Alive: Thanks for the Memories................. 63

9, Hope Alive: My Earth Is Shaking 67

10. Hope Alive: Hung up on a Tree 71

11. Hope Alive: The Mystery of Misery................... 85

Postscript 99

Bibliography 101

Endnotes 105

Introduction:
Theodicy and Godspell

"Though you have made me see troubles, many and bitter, you will restore my life again; from the depths of the earth you will again bring me up." – Psalm 71:20 NIV

Our first understanding of suffering and providence often comes to us through family stories that are passed down. Two of those kinds of stories were passed down to me regarding my great-grandfather, who signed up to serve in World War One with the 2nd Regiment of the Canadian Mounted Rifles in 1914. He did his training in Victoria, British Columbia, and was shipped overseas to France. The night before he was supposed to report to his regiment, he went out with the boys to knock a few back at the pub. He was intoxicated when he returned home. This resulted in him suffering some back problems and being unable to report for military service for eight days. This turned out to be significant for him because the first group of soldiers sent overseas with the Canadian Mounted Rifles were all killed after being gassed by the Germans. My great-grandfather rose to the position of sergeant while serving in France, but his military achievements never eclipsed his memory of a particular event. It occurred when his troop was in a bomb crater in a trench on the battlefront. He wanted more to eat, so he left the crater to get more food. While he was getting his food, the crater was bombed, and all his colleagues were killed. He was the only survivor. I was told by my great-aunt and my grandfather that when my great-grandfather returned from the war, he suffered from post-traumatic stress disorder (PTSD) on account of such experiences. This is perhaps a partial explanation for why he slept in a separate bedroom after the war. It is a providential fact that if my great-grandfather had not survived World War One, my grandfather, my father, myself, my son, and my granddaughter would have never existed. We can live through some very difficult life experiences, and yet we are willed into existence to serve God's multifaceted and cross-generational purposes.

The purpose of this volume is not to plunge into a comprehensive academic and philosophical discussion on the problem of pain, suffering, and evil—also called theodicy. For that, the reader can turn to some books listed in the endnotes.[1] The approach of this volume is more like family and friends sharing around the coffee table some personal experiences and theological reflections on one of the greatest challenges to the Christian faith—the problem of pain and suffering.

In the title of this Introduction, I used the word "Godspell," which in Old English means "good story"[2] and which has come into more modern English as the word "gospel." Those of us who have accepted the gospel of Jesus Christ soon discover that God becomes intimately involved in the stories of our lives as we are drawn into Christ's bigger story (Psalm 139). That means that as Christians we should not be living as if this life is all there is. We live in a certain hope and should be expressing that now.

Another reason I have used the word "Godspell" is that the stories recounted in this volume still evoke a sense of wonder in my mind and remind me why the gospel is so good. The stories in this volume, often dealing with the hard edges of life, are drawn from the stories of my family and from a few of my Sunday sermons; their purpose is to point us in the direction of Who is ultimately good and help us weave our stories into a larger story.

Added to these stories is some theological reflection. It is helpful to remember that life is a journey; we are in process and are being shaped toward a particular end. The stories from my family are likely not that unique, but I hope they will be of some encouragement to others whose own lives are feeling particularly difficult. The things we feel and say and do during tough times can be messy, and God knows that; at such times, He has offered to be a listening ear. The stories in this book reveal God's grace in the midst of hard times. My prayer is that they will help readers to slow their own thoughts down a bit so that they can detect God's small graces that have been sustaining them in their times of desolation. It is necessary to affirm that God is still good and negative circumstances don't change that. It is my hope that readers will find some encouragement in this volume. Hebrews 3:13 instructs us to encourage another, and so we remind each other that God has promised, "I will never desert you, nor will I ever forsake you" (Hebrews 13:5 NASB).

1
Hope Alive: Knock, Knock, Knocking on Heaven's Door

"Oh, the depth of the riches of the wisdom and knowledge of God! How unsearchable his judgments, and his paths beyond tracing out!" – **Romans 11:33 NIV**

For years, one of my spiritual disciplines was to journal my devotional readings and my prayers for various concerns, people, and needs. At the end of the year, I would review all of my journaling and reflect on the themes, answered prayers, and prayers not answered. After more than a decade of praying for some people in particular, I recognized that some prayers for lost or difficult family members had never been answered, at least as far as I could see. This began to make my journaling of certain prayers somewhat disheartening. In fact, I must confess that I was developing a deep sadness over the many unanswered prayers for certain family members. It became a bit depressing to review these repetitious prayers on behalf of people whom I sincerely hoped would come to know Christ in life-giving ways but who seemed no closer to God than when I had begun praying.

It was only gradually that I began to realize that the problem was not with God's failure to answer but with my understanding of prayer. My problem is that I was primarily looking at prayer as a way to get answers to my petitions. Robert Farrar Capon points out, "Answers to prayers for help are a problem only when [we] look on God as a divine vending machine programmed to dispense Cokes... and freedom from [health] trouble to anyone who has the right coins." The reality, Capon explains, is that God's "chief concern is to be himself" to us.[3] Clearly, I had much to learn about prayer. I needed to understand more fully that prayer is not something we use to tell God what to do. Nor is prayer a way we can make deals with God. Prayer is expressing to God the needs we see around us, bringing them before Him, and trusting that He will continue to work mightily in those people's lives. God does not eclipse people's free will and force them to reach out to Him. I have so much to learn about prayer.

Nevertheless, I want to encourage you to never stop praying for people—be it a family member, a friend, or an acquaintance—to come to know Christ. I do not say this because you can know for sure that they *will* become Christians but because you can't know for sure that they *won't* become Christians. We should do this because one thing we do know is that life here on earth will not always go on. Life is all too fragile. The late Steve Jobs, CEO of Apple, once said,

Remembering that I will be dead soon is the most important tool I've ever encountered to help me make the big choices in life. Because almost everything—all external expectations, all pride, all fear of embarrassment or failure—these things just fall away in the face of death, leaving only what is truly important; so, if you live each day as if it were your last, some day you'll most certainly be right.[4]

I could tell you the story about my maternal grandfather coming to Christ late in life. I could tell you the story of my sister being baptized six months before her life ended. Instead, I want to tell you the story of my paternal grandfather.

During my youth and adult years, I constantly prayed for my non-Christian paternal grandfather. He was not a religious person, but, as it is with all of us, my grandfather's everyday life experiences bristled with the need for spiritual reflection. He had existential questions like the rest of us: Who am I? What is the purpose of my life? Does what I do daily have any meaning? What happens when I die? After surviving World War Two, my grandfather lived life without God. Life had been tough, but he was also tough. He rose to become assistant to the chief in his local fire hall. He had become, in his words, a "self-made man." Most people who knew him spoke of my grandfather as an atheist or an agnostic. As far as he knew, the existence of God was either a fiction or something he felt nobody could know.

Then, in 1974, my grandfather got cancer. After his brush with death in 1974, he shifted from being an agnostic to being a deist (someone who believes there is a "Higher Power"). His surgeon said that a Higher Power must have kept my grandfather alive because he should have died. A new understanding was coming out of the brokenness and the messiness of life. When I think of my grandfather at this stage, I think of comedian Lenny Bruce's comment: "Every day people are straying away from the church and going back to God." Not that I completely agree with Bruce, but my grandfather engaged in reflections on Christ, not in a church, but in a hospice room. My grandfather used to say:

> I'm not into religion, but I believe there is a Higher Power outside my conception; I am into spirituality...you feel [that] in your heart; I have felt all my life things have worked out and in many cases almost been handed right to me.

He was referring to the good things that had happened in his life, including his career. I think most of us would feel comfortable with understanding life as a journey, a process in which our understanding of life's meaning evolves. I saw this in Grandpa as he transitioned from an atheist to a deist. After my grandfather's cancer in 1974, he lived life to the full, one day at a time.

What is a deist? Someone who believes that reason and observation of the natural world are sufficient to determine the existence of a Creator (Romans 1:19-20). But it wasn't just the natural world that was influencing my grandfather. Though my grandfather was not religious, he bore the deep imprint of a Protestant work ethic and the Golden Rule drawn from the Christian worldview. It had been in *the air he breathed* growing up as a child. His first impression of the faith came from his mother, who had brought him and the other children to a Baptist church in Vernon, B.C., for a number of years (1927-1931). My grandfather, then aged 8-11, had also witnessed his mother's adult baptism. (Unless your mom is crazy, you'll seriously think about something like that.) His mother remained a believer all her life. My grandfather later spoke fondly of going to his childhood church Sunday school, participating in youth hayrides on Fridays and Saturdays, watching overseas missionaries' slides, and receiving Christmas candies. He also recollected having a role reading a poem during a Christmas play, where he was overcome with giggling in the middle of the program. Over many years in the second half of his life, he attended many Christmas and music programs in churches, most of them at my invitation.

In the chapters of his life when he claimed to have abandoned religion, my grandfather's greatest objections to Christian faith seemed to be concerned with dogmatism and whether there was a God who could be personal with people. It might've taken another lifetime to finally sweat out the answers to those questions. We once discussed "Pascal's wager" during lunch: Pascal argued that it is logical to hedge one's bet—to take a chance on believing in a God who might not exist rather than risk losing eternal happiness by disbelieving in a God who does exist. My sense with Grandpa was that, despite the failings he observed with some people in faith communities, he realized there was something true there, but it needed washing; the dirt needed to be cleaned away, leaving only the eternal. There is a statement that "There are no atheists in foxholes." It is a proverb that suggests that in times of extreme stress or fear, such as when participating in warfare, all people will believe in or hope for a Higher Power. Like all of us, I think that if my grandfather had been convinced there is a good, all-powerful, loving God who can be personally known, then he would have wanted to know Him. And who wouldn't? And yet he was seeing patches of God-light in ordinary things in nature (dogs, a row of flowers, a horse race), in people (family, friends, a wrinkled face, a recovered alcoholic), and the giftedness that had been put into his own life to serve his community.

While my grandfather struggled with terminal cancer his last two years of life, I was burdened in prayer for his soul. During Grandpa's last month of life, I would visit four to five times a week. There were times of deep sharing, saying the important things, such as, "I love you," "Thank you," and "Thanks for serving our country during the war." Sometimes we just held hands.

But I never left without playing some old classic country gospel songs or hymns on my iPhone from the likes of Johnny Cash, Tennessee Ernie Ford, and The Gaithers. I would hold his hand and read sections from the Bible on the love of God, and I would pray with him. (He always said, "Thank you.") One day, I brought him a shelled peanut and told him that, like the peanut, he would leave the shell behind but he would live on in God's love and promises.

On one of those occasions, three weeks before he died, I held his hand and played an iPhone country music version of "The Old Rugged Cross." As he listened to all four verses, he wept very deeply. At first, I thought he was in pain, and I asked him, "Grandpa, what's wrong?"

He couldn't speak for a bit, and then he said, "I want you to have this song sung at my funeral."

A person's reaction to a crisis can be that person's statement of faith. Something had resonated deep within him. Was it a reminder of something he had heard before? A sense of relief or letting go within an old soul? I don't know. But that song had meant enough to him that he requested that it be showcased as an appropriate song for the conclusion of his life. I am left to conclude that he found this song to be the best and final means of expressing his subjective experience in the closing chapter of his life. Did I say, "closing chapter"? If my grandfather did hedge his bet (and I am inclined to believe he did), then this was just the beginning.

About three hours before my grandfather died, I was at his bedside. I was speaking to him, but he was not moving that day. And so I put my iPhone close to his ear and played again that old country tune, "The Old Rugged Cross." He lifted his arm straight up into the air and reached out.

At 7:25 p.m., my grandfather slipped out the back door of this life. He's free now, and my bet is that he knows a freedom that is incomprehensibly complete. My guess is that Grandma has been waiting there for him and has greeted him with the words: "Thank God you took a gamble!"

2

Hope Alive: Humpty Dumpty Had a Great Fall

"A Song of Ascents. I will lift up my eyes to the mountains; from where shall my help come? My help comes from the Lord, who made heaven and earth." – Psalm 121:1-2 NASB

On July 5, 1995, my wife Linda, our four-year-old son, and I had a holiday breakfast at our summer vacation spot—Whistler, British Columbia—and then went biking on the neighboring trails on the north side of the golf course. We were thoroughly enjoying the natural mountain scenery, having fun, and embracing a much-needed break from our normal routines. I was in the lead, with our son in a trailer attached to my bike. We were gliding down a hill when Linda suddenly began frantically screaming my name from behind. By the time I stopped my bike and turned around, I could see my wife skidding down the hill on her face and knees for about three car lengths, with the bike wrapped around her. My son became upset, as I dropped my bike and ran back to her in shock and deep concern. When I rolled her over, I saw she was unconscious and badly scraped on her face, arms, hands, and legs. Because it was early morning, there was no one else in sight. I didn't think there would be many people on the trail, and we were approximately a twenty-minute hike from the closest road. When I saw how deeply Linda's knees and wrists were scraped, I remember thinking that this was really going to hurt. I began to ponder what I was going to do. Left to myself, I most likely would have considered how I could carry my wife down the trail to get her to medical help.

Barely a few minutes had passed when a man approached along the trail and asked, "Can I help?" I answered, "Not unless you're a medical doctor." He told me, "I am a medical doctor."

Neither of us had a cell phone (it was 1995, and cell phones weren't that universal yet). So, I asked if he could attend to my wife while I went down the trail to find someone with a cell phone. Eventually, I came upon some workmen, who called in the emergency and requested an ambulance.

When I returned to my wife and son, the doctor asked, "Did you know she wasn't breathing?" I did not. She had stopped breathing, and I had not recognized it.

Linda became conscious, and she kept asking the same questions over and over. At a minimum, it seemed that she had a bad concussion. The doctor would not allow her to get up, which was a good thing because we later found out she had a skull fracture at the temporal lobe and was hemorrhaging. The presence of this doctor spared me from making some fatal mistakes, such as trying to carry her and causing more rupturing in her brain. The doctor stayed until the ambulance came to pick us up, and then he took our bikes back to the bike rental store. We never did get his name, and we were never able to formally thank him for his exceptional Good Samaritan acts.

When we arrived at Whistler's small hospital, the medical team and physician on duty realized that my wife did not simply have a concussion. The doctor in charge came to meet me in the waiting room and with tears said to me, "I'm sorry. Your wife's condition is deteriorating rapidly, and we don't have the facilities

22

to deal with this. She must be airlifted to Vancouver General Hospital as soon as possible." The physician urged that when the helicopter came, I should accompany my wife to Vancouver. They told me that they were doing everything they could to locate the first available medical helicopter but it would take some time for the helicopter to come from Vancouver. However, it happened that a helicopter had just been fueled up in Vancouver and was free to come, which would save my wife precious time and perhaps her life or at least save her from severe brain damage. There was certainly a transcendent quality to all of this; people seldom believe in miracles until they need one.

Despite the physician's urging, I did not go on the helicopter, as I had my son with me and I needed to return to the condo to pack up our vacation items to head back home. A social worker kindly drove me and my son all the way to Vancouver General Hospital (VGH). On the way, from time to time my son would say things like, "Daddy, Mommy didn't fall off a bike. Mommy didn't have an accident." In hindsight, I realize I was still in shock during that hour and forty minute drive from Whistler to Vancouver.

At the hospital, we were met by various members of our family, a social worker, and two clergy. I couldn't look my mother-in-law in the face, as I could see how devastated she was. She needed her own personal social worker, and I was busy trying to keep my emotions together. Our happy vacation had turned into a very dark experience.

Shortly after arrival, I was ushered into a conference room with the assisting neurosurgeon, the social worker, a nurse, and some others. A top, internationally known neurosurgeon, Dr. Felix Durity, had performed the operation; the hospital had called him back from the beginning of his holiday to deal with my wife's case. I was told bluntly that

Linda's fall had caused a skull fracture that had severed a major artery and caused a hemorrhage in the brain. To relieve the pressure, they had performed a craniotomy, cutting an opening in the skull the size of a tea cup saucer. I was also told that her brain was bruised and was continuing to swell and that they were fighting to keep her alive. The doctors could not guarantee her life; at this point, they were fighting to stabilize the pressure inside her skull. If she could survive past the next three to five days, then they would consider the possible outcomes, which could include paralysis, brain damage, and cognitive decrements. The key point was that they could not guarantee her life. She had fractures in the cheek, nose, skull, pelvis, and hip. She seemed to have broken everything but her nails.

This was a bit heavy. I would later become aware that our pastor had informed a prayer chain group regarding my wife's accident. One man in that congregation did not know about the accident, but reported he had woken up in the middle of the night, burdened to pray for my wife. The leaders of my in-laws' Italian church stopped their plans for a service and simply called the congregation to pray for her life. Some from that church informed people in Italy, who also began petitioning in prayer.

I spent the next three days sleep deprived near my wife while she was in the Intensive Care Unit. Her head swelled up like a beach ball, to the point that I did not recognize her face. They were keeping her body cool to inhibit swelling, and she had tubes for drainage coming out of the top of her skull. At the time of this accident, I was a graduate student. I began seriously considering quitting the program, given the need to reevaluate my priorities.

On day three, I went to visit a physician-counselor regarding whether I should be preparing for a funeral or preparing for all of the aftermath that could come with a head injury. I remember the counselor sharing with me his own loss of a child that had been stillborn; his wife had been so shaken up that she had left him. It had been a double loss for him—but he said what had helped him make it through was refocusing on being thankful to God for the good things that he had enjoyed prior to the losses. His counsel to me was: if she dies, be thankful to God for the good times that you have shared together. I took his counsel to heart.

By this time, family members were telling me that there was something emotionally the matter with my son. During those first three days, he had been staying with his grandparents. Because he had seen his mother's accident, he had been traumatized. This had manifested itself in extreme behavior, anger, and nightmares. He would cry out at night, calling for his mother. After three days, I took my son home with me, and on the morning of the following day I tried to tell him what had happened to his mother. As soon as I said, "Your mom has had an accident," he bolted across the hallway and ran into his room, crying, "I want my mommy, I want my mommy." I went in after him and held him. We both wept, and I prayed while holding him. This was a dark time for us.

On the fifth day, my wife woke up, just at the time her Italian aunt and mother came into the hospital room. Her aunt addressed her in Italian, and her mom addressed her in French. When I heard my wife reply in both languages, I knew this was a good start. However, our son would not see his mother for nearly two weeks, partly because he had gotten sick from the stress. When I would go to see her, he would say, "Tell Mama I love her and I want to marry her."

On day eleven, my wife was released from the hospital. Her survival and recovery, having all the fragrance of providence, was being described as a miracle.[5] Linda's healing process would take three years, using the resources of medicine, clinical counseling, journaling, and the support of our faith community. My son would also need counseling as a result of having witnessed the bloody accident. Providentially, I was enabled to generate high sales commissions at my day job, and we did not lose our house.

Questions

Something about this incident left me with lingering thoughts that have taken some time to be formulated into questions. My first question was: if God could perform a miracle—the unexpected arrival of the doctor, the availability of a speedy helicopter, and the fact that there was no brain damage in the final outcome—why didn't He just spare us the pain of the accident entirely? Why didn't He just back up the miracle by a few minutes? It seemed an unanswerable question. The second question was: why would such a loving and good God permit my wife to experience excruciating physical pain, permit my little son to experience trauma, and allow me to experience psychological and emotional pain and stress?

Paul Brand observed that North Americans' love affair with the pursuit of happiness means that we are far less equipped to handle suffering than people from other times and places and we are far more traumatized by it. Our culture's conventional wisdom is out of step with a theologically orthodox view of pain and pleasure.[6]

The experience of uncertainty and pain drives people to religion and philosophy to find an explanation. Warren Wiersbe points out that when life hands us unexpected pain, we start to ask questions such as "Why me?" In fact, he continues, we tend to forget that "the Bible is filled with complaints of ill-treatment...a persistent chorus of 'how could you do this to me?' And yet God never apologizes nor explains."[7] Our incident seemed so random, so pointless, so obviously a product of mere chance, I resonated with the words of Peter Kreeft, "Where is God in all this?"[8] Never had I found it so difficult to pray as when I was in the midst of my wife's head injury crisis. Kreeft comments that no one after repeated shocks turns easily to God and smiles. He tells the story of Teresa of Avila being thrown from her carriage. According to a report, she questioned God, and He answered her, "This is how I treat all my friends." Her reply was, "Then Lord, it is not surprising that you have so few."[9] C.S. Lewis stated, "Pain insists upon being attended to. God whispers to us in our pleasures, speaks in our conscience, but shouts in our pain; it is His megaphone to rouse a deaf world."[10] My wife's incident completely interrupted our flow of life, leaving us to ponder what seemed to be the mystery of suffering in a God-made and God-ruled universe. Lewis commented:

> Christianity, in a sense, creates, rather than solves the problem of pain, for pain would be no problem unless, side by side with our daily experience of this painful world, we had received what we think a good assurance that ultimate reality is righteous and loving. To become a Christian is to have the problem of pain.[11]

Some atheistic thinkers, such as Friedrich Nietzsche and Richard Rorty, argue that it is unnecessary to bring God into the discussion—there is no overriding purpose or meaning to the narratives of humans' lives, only ever-present chance.[12]

My starting point for addressing the problem of pain is Christian faith, God's revelation in the Bible, and my own experience with God. My intention is not to solve the problem of pain in this chapter, but to show the direction in which a solution might lie.

At this point, I think it would be helpful to restate the essential question that arises when people encounter painful life events. C.S. Lewis phrased the question this way:

> If God were good, he would wish to make his creatures perfectly happy, and if God were almighty, he would be able to do what he wished. But the creatures are not happy, therefore God lacks either goodness, or power, or both. This is the problem of pain in its simplest form.[13]

Adapting this question to my wife's accident, I could ask: why couldn't an all-powerful God entirely spare our family the pain of my wife's accident?

1. Human Freedom and Frailty

Norman Geisler commented that evil cannot be destroyed without destroying freedom. Free beings are the cause of evil, and freedom was given to us so that we could love. But love is impossible without freedom. So, if freedom were destroyed, it would deprive creatures of their greatest good. Herbert Carson pointed out that because of the fall, human beings are alienated from God and their minds are darkened; he said that human beings are impaired, having imperfections and limited judgments. Augustine held that evil represents the going wrong of something good.[14] This suggests that evil events such as the tragedy that hit our family are simply due to human frailty, human miscalculation, or even mechanical failure. An environment intended to make growth possible in free beings must operate according to general and dependable laws that involve real dangers, difficulties, problems, obstacles, and the possibility of pain, failure, sorrow, and frustration.[15]

2. God's Goodness

Why would a loving and good God allow my wife to experience excruciating physical pain, not to mention the emotional pain that befell our entire family? Is there something capricious about God? René Descartes affirmed that there is no aberration in God's nature and that He is unquestionably good.[16] Gottfried Leibniz affirmed that we cannot rightly judge evil if we consider only the particular evil thing or event. Some things in themselves appear to be evil but turn out to be prerequisites for good.[17] C.S. Lewis pointed out that if God is wiser than we are, His judgment must differ from ours on many things, not least on good and evil. What seems to us good may therefore not be good in God's eyes, and what seems to us evil may not be evil. Lewis suggested that God is maintaining order in the universe even when we human beings conclude something has gone wrong. The problem is that humans reduce God's love to something trivial such as kindness when God is actually in the process of making something of us and that creative process includes the cross.[18]

There is a widespread assumption among philosophers in particular that human happiness is what is most important. For example, Aristotle held that happiness is goodness (feeling good).[19] John Locke said that things are good or evil only in reference to pleasure or pain—what we call good should increase our pleasure and diminish our pain.[20] Thomas Hobbes noted that people call good whatever they love and evil whatever they hate because they are chiefly concerned with their own survival.[21] Albert Camus and Jean-Paul Sartre asserted that the only wrong is that which produces pain or inconvenience.[22] But, in many instances, God's notion of good and humans' perspective on what is good can be polar opposites.

C.S. Lewis suggested that when we want to be something other than what God wants us to be, we must be wanting what in fact will not make us happy; God intends to give us what we need, not what we think we want.[23]

3. God's Purposes

In terms of purpose, the philosopher Bertrand Russell called human beings a curious accident in a backwater.[24] In contrast, the Bible indicates that the God of Abraham, Isaac, and Jacob has deep purposes for the universe He created and for human beings. However, there is a huge difference between God having a purpose for allowing evil and our knowing what that purpose is. When it comes to the problem of suffering, we should "treat it as a mystery to be entered, not as a puzzle to be solved."[25] We cannot assume there is no good purpose for something just because we don't know what it could be.[26] The really big question is not why we experience suffering but what the purpose of life is.[27] Gottfried Leibniz compared life to looking at only part of a painting that is mostly covered; he said it is not proper for us to judge unless we have examined the whole, but we know only a very small part of immeasurable eternity.[28]

Suffering may accomplish many things. For me and my family, it caused us to be more appreciative of life, of each other, and of the journey we share. Others who were touched by my wife's misery were awakened from living superficially and moved to prayer. I sensed that many of us were being conformed just a little more into the image of Christ (Romans 8:29). I sensed that God was unceasingly involved in the process. But while we caught glimpses of God's purposes in allowing my wife's accident, there was very much that remained a mystery.

Warren Wiersbe's insight into this issue is instructive. He says that when we hurt deeply, what we really need is not an explanation from God but a revelation of God; we need to see how great God is and recover our lost perspective in life.[29] In other words, pain can be transformational even while we remain in the dark about why some things happened as they did.

The bottom line is that there will remain a lot of unsolvable mysteries due to our limited understanding about God. Good people face hardships too, and we can't depend on our ability to comprehend the inexplicable; we simply haven't been given enough facts to explain all the heartache.[30] The Bible shows clearly that suffering is part of the human condition; we all must endure some things that bring pain, discomfort, and sorrow, and we need to accept that these burdens are ours to carry. Our lives are influenced by forces that are beyond the scope of our understanding; our task is not to try to explain the inexplicable but to remain faithful and obedient to Him who knows all mysteries.[31]

3
Hope Alive: After the Pink Slip

"'For I know the plans that I have for you,' declares the Lord, 'plans for welfare and not for calamity, to give you a future and a hope.'" – Jeremiah 29:11 NASB

Late in 1996, the national company for which I had worked for nearly eleven years experienced what would be later recognized as a hostile corporate takeover. Immediately, the new corporation discontinued various perks that had greatly contributed to employee morale. Without warning, events such as employee picnics, Christmas parties, and children's Easter egg hunts had become a thing of the past.

The new national company offered employees an option to invest in its stocks and encouraged us to continue to purchase its products—in spite of the fact that this company was well known for practices such as ferocious downsizing, permanent plant closures, and elimination of jobs.

Within the next few months, the new corporate owners of our organization had laid off the entire administration department, contracting out the work, and had fully computerized the sales division. The remaining departments, composed of unionized members, were lulled into a false sense of security, based on assurances that the new ownership would honor the collective agreement. Employees planned their finances, purchases, and mortgages based on that false sense of security. Then, in February of 1997, the head office notified the union membership that a section of the collective agreement had "fuzzy language" which would allow the company to break the assumed terms of the contract. The corporation's lawyers had found a loophole, and the corporation was determined to exploit it. The union membership was stunned, shocked, and horrified at the implications of this announcement. In order to avoid an expensive, losing legal battle, the employees' union abandoned its members. All employees in the production department with less than ten years of service were laid off. We all felt like David up against Goliath, except we didn't have a slingshot or a stone. The company at the time of the takeover had 350 employees, many of whom had given their full careers to this organization. Within a year, the company reduced and downsized to around 175 employees.

Besides the dismissal of the administration department, as a head of health and safety for the sales division, I became aware of many other individuals facing hardships. The majority of the sales division were family men with mortgages and children to support. Some were single parents, and some were older employees who would face age discrimination issues in seeking to be employed elsewhere. Many of my colleagues were becoming emotionally disturbed over the pending disruption of their lives and the prospect of having to start over again and seek another job. I was made aware of escalating drug and alcohol use, negative behavior, problems in some employees' relationships and home lives, and rising levels of absenteeism (there was an unprecedented volume of sick, WorkSafe, and stress leaves). I witnessed some of my male colleagues get wet in the eyes as they grieved the impending loss of their jobs. I could see disappointment, disorientation, and discouragement in them as they desperately tried to cling to their self-respect. As a way of expressing their anger, some men in the production department sabotaged some of the production equipment. Unfortunately, this simply led to the company installing surveillance cameras and threatening to bring criminal charges. The downsizing process took about one year to complete, and during that time the work environment became very negative and toxic. Some workers had become increasingly vulgar, almost as if they had undergone a personality change as a result of stress. Some men stopped shaving or cutting their hair, neglecting to groom themselves in a manner appropriate for a marketplace sales division. One of my colleagues suffered a nervous breakdown; another colleague had a heart attack; a supervisor suffered heart and chest pains after he witnessed two other supervisors being laid off. Three marriages collapsed in the sales division during this period of downsizing.

The company's sales dropped eighteen percent in just twelve months. By June of 1998, the company's sales had dropped between twenty and thirty percent.

The takeover affected me in a direct way when the employees in the sales division were notified that the company would be contracting out (franchising) our jobs. If we wanted to remain employed with the company, we would have to come up with $120,000 to $150,000 to buy a franchise (a sales territory with existing accounts). I would have to buy a five-ton truck and work a seven-day week (or train and pay someone to cover for me when I needed to take a day off). The franchise could only be bought and held for a year at a time, and then the terms would have to be renegotiated, even though most of the salesmen would have to spread their financing over a five-year period. The commissions would also be restructured, meaning that the new contract workers would be working for less, in addition to receiving no benefits. When the salesmen approached independent accountants to assess the value of the franchises, the accountants unanimously said the franchises were high risk and overpriced, being worth only about $50,000. It was becoming apparent that the corporation was taking advantage of economic conditions in order to drive down employee compensation and increase profits for the stockholders.

Of an original sales force of eighty, I would eventually be one of the last remaining four or five company employees. I survived as a relief sales driver covering the unsold sales routes. About ninety percent of the sales route franchises were purchased by people from outside the company; these people bought themselves a job while knowing next to nothing about the company's industry or marketplace. The sales knowledge, history, and talent of my former colleagues had all been discarded within a period of a year. The sober realization dawned on many of my colleagues that their years of service and loyalty had counted for nothing. I was a last representative of a dying culture. It was difficult to watch and more difficult to be a part of.

The experience raised a lot of questions for me.

Why didn't I buy a sales franchise? The first obstacle was this company's ethics. This corporate giant had already broken one contract (the collective agreement with its unionized employees), and I could not trust it enough to enter into a deeper contractual relationship where I would be incurring all the expenses and bearing all the risks. In addition, I recognized that these new franchise contracts allowed the company to move the goalposts of the commissions or take away accounts at its discretion. There was no protection for the franchisee.

Being caught in an organizational downsizing is not an easy situation to deal with. But it is a situation that many people are facing or will face in the future. The reality of global economics is that many jobs get farmed out overseas. And companies and organizations in all sectors use periodic downsizing to remain competitive. Capitalism has always had a dark side when its practices come into conflict with values, principles, and ethics.

As important as these topics are, this book is not about economics and business practices. Rather, my focus here is on those experiencing downsizing or job loss. People in these situations often feel the temptation to withdraw from community and succumb to depression or a negative state of mind. In light of this temptation, I deeply resonate with W.H. Vanstone's focus on the importance of the church in "sustaining the life of the community."[32]

When facing job loss, what is especially needed is to strengthen our understanding of our identity in Christ. It is so tempting to see our work as what gives us meaning, identity, self-worth, and core satisfaction. It is crucial to understand that our true vocation is that of being Christ followers and our employment is just one of the assignments that are allotted to us according to the common grace we have been given. Downsizing and unemployment force us to reevaluate our thinking in this matter and strengthen our other relationships of family, church, and community.

I won't pretend that I didn't struggle with a measure of anxiety about carrying a mortgage and supporting my family when my employment future was so uncertain. There would be a few hiccups and false starts before I settled again into another stable employment arrangement. In hindsight, what I discovered was that the experience challenged me to pray and to reevaluate where I was placing my security and identity. God was faithful in helping me meet my economic obligations throughout the transition process. It is easy to cite overly optimistic sayings such as, "The closing of one chapter means the opening of another." But I was seriously pressed to think biblically about who really helped me to pay my bills and put food on my table. This was not entirely a bad thing in a culture where people see themselves as "self-made." My conclusion is Jesus is the same yesterday, today, and tomorrow. He is forever faithful.

4
Hope Alive: The Big Bang Theory

"As I walked out of the door toward the gate that would lead to my freedom, I knew if I didn't leave my hatred and bitterness behind, I'd still be in prison." – Nelson Mandela

On October 8, 2007, Thanksgiving Day, our extended family had planned a Thanksgiving dinner for 6:00 p.m. The weather was bright, and the sun was warm and forgiving. My wife and I had gone out for coffee and a muffin at Calabria Café on Commercial Drive in Vancouver's Little Italy and had done some shopping. While we were returning home, we received a phone call telling us that our son was in Royal Columbian Hospital and we needed to get there quickly. We weren't told what had happened, so I was left to speculate. Maybe our son had fallen down the stairs or done something clumsy; after all, he was a developing sixteen-year-old with size thirteen shoes.

We arrived at the hospital to find a police officer present and our son waiting for surgery to remove metal from his neck. We were completely shocked to find out what had led up to this situation.

Apparently, our son had been randomly terrorized and violently assaulted. Our son had been waiting at the bus stop across the street from our home. While neighbors were cutting their lawns and playing with their kids outside, a carload of three older teens came slowly cruising through the area. Our son later told us that he didn't like the way that they were looking at him while he was standing at the bus stop. He felt intimidated. Then the car turned around and accelerated towards our son. The occupants rolled down the windows of the car, pulled out two Walther P99 replica pellet guns, and began firing shots (steel pellets, the kind that are often used to kill birds or squirrels) into the body of our son. One of the pellets penetrated his neck. He realized he had been hit when he placed his hand on his neck and the hand became covered in blood.

As the perpetrators were speeding away, one of the neighbors identified several digits from the car license plate and noted the color and make of the vehicle. Our son used his cell phone to call 911 and notify the police that he had just been shot. Because the police detachment is near our home, the police were able to deploy a helicopter and several police cars very quickly. The carload of perpetrators were swiftly apprehended about 1.5 kilometers away by several constables with guns drawn. It was later reported that this incident cost the City nearly a million dollars in resources.

Our son waited about an hour to get a simple surgery and five stitches—he was most fortunate that the pellet had missed his jugular, though just barely. But that was the easiest part of the ordeal to get over. Our son managed to join the family for Thanksgiving dinner that night—although he was still emotionally numb—and we most certainly thanked God that nothing *physically* worse had come out of this incident.

I wish I could say the story ended there and we all lived happily ever after. It didn't!

Within a couple of days, our son broke down in tears, and then he began to express deep hurt and anger over the incident. His emotional condition began to spill over into his other relationships and into his capacity to undertake normal activities. He was having difficulties concentrating at school, and he struggled with paranoia when he was walking on the streets, waiting at a bus stop, or taking public transit. I had to drive him to and from school every day. Unfortunately, he still could not cope, and he blew the entire semester at school. School authorities indicated that his post-traumatic stress was more than the capabilities of the school counselors to deal with. So, our son was placed into therapy with a specialist who dealt with violent assaults of this nature. This was a very messy season in the life of our son and in the life of our family.

Our son was so angry, he just wanted to legally charge the guys who had shot him. Given the stage of moral development most teens are at, his feelings were to be expected.

We were advised to take the route of *restorative justice.* This would mean that our son (and our family) would face the three perpetrators (and their families) in an extended meeting. The perpetrators would be expected to offer public apologies and do community service. The goal would be to bring some understanding, resolution, closure, and healing to all those involved.

One of the hardest issues we discussed with our son during this period was the concept of forgiveness. At one opportune moment, we talked with him about the Parable of the Unmerciful Servant (Matthew 18:21-35). We told him that practicing forgiveness was an important part of our faith and our worldview. We didn't pretend that putting that concept into practice would be easy, but we assured him that it was necessary in order for him to be able to move on. Sadly, our son was getting quite different messages from his friends, who were planting ideas of revenge, retaliation, and "getting even" in his mind. He also experienced some teens at school teasing him by shaping their hands like a gun, pointing at him, and saying, "Bang." At first, he refused to go into a restorative justice circle to bring closure to the matter.

However, after nearly four months of therapy, some time away from school, and time to reflect, he became ready to face the three perpetrators. After this, we were thankful that our son returned to school in a more peaceful frame of mind and showed a good deal of progress through a difficult emotional process. I don't think he will ever forget the experience, but today he does realize that it could have been far more serious. He has expressed that he is aware of God's providence at work in this situation.

My guess is that many reading this story will not have had a very similar experience, but many may have experienced being violated in other ways. Life can be very messy, and it may be difficult to talk about what's going on in a family's home while things are still quite frayed. As a pastor during this event, there were a lot of details I couldn't discuss publicly; it was tough trying to have some privacy while living in a fish bowl. Getting our emotions to line up with our beliefs can take time. Healing takes time. But I have witnessed in our own home, by God's grace, that a day can arrive when healing is in evidence. We have chosen to call it Thanksgiving Day.

5
Hope Alive: It Comes in Threes

"There is a time for everything, and a season for every activity under the heavens...a time to weep...a time to mourn." – Ecclesiastes 3:1,4 NIV

"In this world you will have trouble. But take heart! I have overcome the world." – John 16:33 NIV

Up to this point in my life, I had not experienced much in the way of grieving the loss of loved ones. All that would change on Tuesday, February 23, 2010. I received a 6:00 a.m. phone call from my healthy, 90-year-old grandfather indicating that my grandmother had died of a sudden heart attack.

Because the rest of my family live out of town, I spent the rest of the day with my grandfather, helping him write an obituary for the paper and preparing the eulogy. My grandfather didn't want a stranger doing the funeral of my grandma, so he asked me to do it. Preparing for the funeral would take eight days, and it was one of the hardest things I have ever done. I would end up being responsible for preparing all parts of the community funeral—the eulogy, the message, and the photo and music tribute. I prayed that God would give me strength to stay steady for the family and community guests as I honored her life. I was also the one responsible for phoning the rest of the family with the news. My sister indicated that she would come to Canada's west coast for the funeral by the end of the week. I had been close to my grandparents, so all of this was tough, but as the week progressed, I felt we would get through it.

Then, around 6:00 a.m. on Sunday, February 28, I received another phone call from my grandfather. He said, "I'm afraid I've got more bad news. Your sister has been murdered." I couldn't believe my ears. But, at 7:00 a.m., the local police came to deliver this very same news to my home. This was a shock. My sister was supposed to have come from another province for Grandma's funeral, and she didn't make it. Again I found myself in the position of having to deliver the bad news to other family members. Apparently, a couple of people had broken into my sister's home, and things had gone terribly wrong—she had lost her life in a horrific scuffle. I prepared another DVD with a photo and music tribute for my sister's memorial as a way of honoring her life. I had thought that we would have been able to grow old together, laugh, and reminisce.

At 4:30 p.m. on Saturday March 6, 2010, I received a third phone call, informing me that my wife's aunt, who had been close to our family, had just succumbed to a rapid cancer. We were shocked. The news brought one more wave of discouragement to our family.

Grieving over one person can be tough, but grieving over three in 13 days was even more complex. Our son became deeply upset and almost fearfully superstitious. We all felt walloped emotionally, like we had been hit three times by trucks while crossing the road. I was in a fog. The emotional state of the entire family was something I don't have words for. I pondered Psalm 77:1-20, particularly verses 2 and 4: "My soul refused to be comforted...I am so troubled that I cannot speak" (NASB). Exhaustion, tears, sadness, and moments of numbness filled many of those days, and nothing was bringing relief. I will not compare our family's losses to those Job suffered, but I certainly identified with Job 2:13 (NIV): "Then [Job] sat on the ground…for seven days and seven nights. No one said a word to him, because they saw how great his suffering was." Several family members were slipping into depression over what had just happened. My grandfather's health and emotional state began to seriously decline. He suffered from digestive problems and internal bleeding. I remember my grandfather saying, "This is the worst thing that's ever happened to the family."

I quickly became too tired to do ministry (at the time, I was working as an associate pastor). I felt I had nothing to give. After ten days, I did try to go in to the office—at the urging of the church board and the lead pastor—but I felt so depressed I couldn't concentrate on my work. I remember weeping at my computer terminal listening to Nat King Cole's song, "Smile though your heart is breaking." After thirteen days away, I finally returned to work full time. But I had lost interest in the things that I'd previously been passionate about—music, reading, community service, and study. A lot of the joy, energy, and motivation had been sucked out of me. I simply longed for solitude. I don't think I have ever felt this sad. There were so many things that triggered memories of the deceased, their faces, and the sound of their voices. Grief can be a wolf and catch us unaware. I felt as if I was suffocating both at work and at home. Sometimes at night, when I tried to sleep, my chest ached.

At the same time, we were very appreciative of our church family. Many gave comforting words, cards, flowers, and caring hugs at a time when we were in a mystified fog of grief. Our living room looked and smelled like a florist shop.

Death has an incredible ability to wipe away the fictions that we can be living in—revealing the lack of stewardship with our lives, our forgetfulness that we are mortal, our preoccupation with our personal ambitions. Certainly, I had not been giving much attention to the fact that death is the final enemy we all will face. There are many Bible texts that I think we need to ponder more carefully than we do, such as Luke 12:20 (NIV): "This very night your life will be demanded from you..." Remarkably, there have been moments during my grieving when I have felt God palpably close to His creation. I recognized that it was He who had been the Sovereign over the number of days that my grandmother, sister, and aunt-in-law lived (Psalm 139:16). I must say that this has helped me to realize more and more that God is to be revered. When we die, our eulogies will sum up our entire lives and all of our accomplishments in about 15 to 30 minutes, but what will really count is whether we chose to follow Christ or not. There is some consolation for me that my three family members all died in Christ; for that I am eternally grateful. At the same time, I believe we need to see our lives through the lens of the scriptures; one thing we might learn is how uninformed some parts of our lives can be when they are not directed by God's Word. I am reminded of how important it is for us to tell the other people in our lives that we love them—knowing that it may be our last opportunity to do so.

Through the process of grieving, I've turned over many questions in my mind that seem to have no answers. One in particular stands out: why my family? I have found myself wrestling with how to connect God and the suffering of an innocent person. I re-examined again and again my views on the mercy and justice of God. While questioning God during this time, I found some helpful words in Barbara Brown Taylor's book, *When God is Silent:*

God never does answer Job's question. Job's question was about justice. God's answer is about omnipotence, and as far as I know that is the only reliable answer human beings have ever gotten about why things happen the way they do. God only knows. And we are not God. When the dust settles...Job admits, "I have spoken of the unspeakable and tried to grasp the infinite."[33]

At the time I wrote about these events, I was aware that our family was still working through the stages of grief. Our losses have been deep, some days have been better than others, and we have been grateful for the support we have received from our church family. I have also discovered that there is a lot of helpful material on working through grief. One book I would highly recommend, especially to those who have lost a sibling, is *Surviving the Death of a Sibling: Living through Grief When an Adult Brother or Sister Dies* by T.J. Wray.[34]

6
Hope Alive: It's Murder

*"When Jesus saw her, he called her forward and said to her,
'Woman, you are set free from your infirmity.'"*
– Luke 13:12 NIV

Nothing will ever describe the shock and pain I felt the day I received an early morning phone call from my grandfather and then a visit from Victim Services, telling me that my sister had been murdered. What followed was a grief journey that was confusing, disorienting, and disruptive to our regular rhythm of life.

I've come to realize that many people we know will not understand the personal feelings of loss we are experiencing, and at times we may feel that they are failing at being supportive. After about eight days of being off work, I remember people asking me if I was doing better—as if I had had the flu or something. There are some people who think that grief is something we must hurry through. However, I am thankful for those who shared a hug, a card, or flowers—and there were many.

What I was not prepared for was the roller coaster of grief. It would hit me when I least expected it, triggered by a song, a sight, a place, a memory. I can remember weeping a lot. I had a constant feeling of exhaustion and depression—all normal, given the abnormal circumstances.

Those who find themselves in a place like this should not rule out the value of a good counselor and/or consulting a physician for medication if necessary. After all, we are living in the 21st century, and we should realize the value of these professions to our emotional health.

It took me about five months to come to a place where I found a new normal. During that time, I remember replaying dreams about my sister's last moments leading up to her murder. There were constant reminders that she was gone, and there was nothing that anybody could do about it. I must confess that I struggled with the idea that God was being unjust in allowing her to be murdered. I came to recognize that grieving this kind of loss is a manifestation of how much we cared for and loved the person we lost. Any time we grieve the loss of a family member's life, we are reminded of the fragility of our own lives here on earth. These are times we need to turn to God, who is eager to share our moments and touch us with His comfort. In my time of grief, I found comfort in various passages of Scripture:

> The Lord is my shepherd; I shall not want. He makes me lie down in green pastures; He leads me beside quiet waters. He restores my soul. He guides me in the paths of righteousness for His name's sake. Even though I walk through the valley of the shadow of death, I fear no evil, for You are with me; Your rod and Your staff, they comfort me. (Psalm 23:1-4 NASB)

> God is our refuge and strength, a very present help in trouble. (Psalm 46:1 NASB)

> The Lord is near to all who call upon Him,
> To all who call upon Him in truth.
> He will fulfill the desire of all who fear Him;

He will also hear their cry and will save them.
(Psalm 145:18-19 NASB)

I also found comfort in Christian writings, such as this prayer from Victor D. Lehman's book, *The Pastor's Guide to Weddings & Funerals*:

> Thank you, gracious God, for your comforting presence. Thank you for wrapping your arms of unconditional love around us and filling us with your peace, even as we have grieved the loss of our loved one. Thank you for the extra portion of comfort and strength you give for such a time as this. Eternal God, we praise you for this one, whom you graciously gave life. Let your everlasting light shine on them. And help us so to believe where we have not seen, that your presence may lead us through our years, and bring us at last into the joy of your home not made with hands, but eternal in the heavens. Through Jesus Christ our Lord we pray.

I also found comfort, as well as pain, in remembering my sister. From as far back as I can remember, my sister stuck her chin out to life, as if she were saying, "Here I am, world." There were many sides to my sister's life, but in essence she was a good-hearted person. I can remember that as a kid she was thoughtful of others; she bought unselfish Christmas gifts. I can remember a time when I was in grade four and some other kid was pounding the daylights out of me. She came along, pushed the watching kids aside, and yelled, "That's my brother!" She then grabbed the guy by the hair and finished off the fight. My earliest memory of her is sharing toys with her at Christmas when we were kids. One Christmas in the early 1960s, I remember taking the chocolate-colored doll she had received and making it mine, while she took the teddy bear that had been intended for me.

My sister's teen years could be summed up as "storm and stress"—she was the storm, and others felt the stress. My sister was headstrong as a teenager and seemed to be able to laugh about that. She was drawn to the arts. Had she benefited from a college education in theatre or acting, I think she could have built a career in that area. However, like most of us, she married, which led to her becoming a stepmother. My sister lived life and brought life; if she was in a room, everyone there knew it. She loved being with people, and people mostly enjoyed being with her. My sister had a big laugh (actually kind of a cackle) and a knack for wearing bright, even loud, clothing.

In the last five days of my sister's life, she was grieving the loss of our grandmother. When I called her on Tuesday, February 23 to tell her that our grandmother had passed away, she took it hard. She had been planning to make it out to the west coast to see Grandma one last time and say her goodbyes while Grandma was in the long-term hospital. My sister pleaded with me to pray with her on the phone, but I was so choked up by the news that I couldn't get a word out. That morning, she called her grandfather six times, and the two of them grieved together.

My sister called me again on Wednesday, February 24 to tell me she was getting a plane ticket and would be with us by Friday. I had to attend a study conference at Seattle Pacific University in Washington State that Friday and Saturday, so Grandpa was waiting for the phone call from my sister to say that she had arrived. But she didn't call. We thought that she had simply been delayed, which was okay because Grandma's funeral wasn't scheduled until Wednesday. We could never have guessed why she didn't make it. At 8:30 p.m. on Saturday, February 27, two armed men broke into my sister's home and shot her to death.

I remember feeling an intense amount of pain and anger over this. Suffering the loss of someone we love can be the most difficult thing in life to deal with. One moment we have them, and the next they're gone. What are we supposed to do? How are we supposed to feel? The truth is that there's no one way that we're "supposed" to feel. Whatever we're feeling is okay. It's okay to feel shock, anger, denial, or whatever else we may feel. It's okay. And if we don't feel anything at all, that's okay too. It's okay to have no answers and no explanations. Because sometimes all the reasoning and comforting words in the world just aren't what we need.

My sister went out of life the way she came into life—with a bang. She always had a lot of things on the go. She was a locomotive, someone who loved plants, cats, fitness, and the latest diet. In confronting the separation that her death had brought, there were precious memories such as these that will last forever in my heart. These memories are a living testament of a person who sought to live life with enthusiasm. My life has been richer for having known her. There was another prayer from Victor D. Lehman's book that I found helpful in this regard:

> O God, who gave us life, in whom we live and move and have our being…You are ever more ready to hear than we are to pray. You know our needs before we ask, and you know the things that can hinder us in asking. Give to us now your grace, that as we shrink before the mystery of death, we may see the light of eternity. Speak to us once more your solemn message of life and of death. Help us to live as those who are prepared to die. And when our days here are accomplished, enable us to die

as those who go forth to live, so that living or dying, our life may be in you, and that nothing in life or in death will be able to separate us from your great love in Jesus Christ our Lord.[35]

It is God, our Father, who comforts us in our loss. And it is God, our Father, whom we should thank for the gift of life and all that makes life precious and worth living. We should thank Him for choosing to place us in families. We should thank Him for the great friends who come to stand beside us to strengthen our spirits and enlarge our vision. Life is precious, and a family death reminds us how great a gift life really is. At such times, we realize that our bodies were not made to last forever. They grow weary and become worn out. We should also thank God that, in His design, there is a provision for that time when our days are spent and that we can be released from these earthly forms, freed from the limitations and weaknesses of the body. For that reason, we can thank our Lord for our loved ones who have experienced this release, even if it has happened tragically.

7
Hope Alive: This Is Mental

"There are no ordinary people. You have never talked to a mere mortal. Nations, cultures, arts, civilizations—these are mortal, and their life is to ours as the life of a gnat. But it is immortals whom we joke with, work with, marry, snub and exploit—immortal horrors or everlasting splendors. This does not mean that we are to be perpetually solemn. We must play. But our merriment must be of that kind (and it is, in fact, the merriest kind) which exists between people who have, from the outset, taken each other seriously—no flippancy, no superiority, no presumption." – C.S. Lewis, The Weight of Glory

I remember being a part of a church where the pastor welcomed the request of a Christian social worker to bring several mentally challenged adults to the Sunday services. At times, these individuals would speak and behave in inappropriate ways during the worship and the preaching. Yet their presence was a major statement by the pastor about the value that God places on people who are made in the image of God. It required the congregation to be more accommodating with weaker members in the faith community.

Sadly, I think that most churches have people in them who make some other people feel uncomfortable, often to the point that they wish they could send them away. I knew a pastor whose teenage child had mental health issues. He said that a deacon had asked him to send his child away to attend another church. The pastor felt deeply hurt by the request.

At times, I have witnessed the enormous discouragement that strikes couples and families with a family member who suffers with mental health issues. The struggle is very real whether the family member with the mental health issues is an elderly parent, a spouse, a teenager, a child, or a member of the extended family. I remember visiting with a church family who had a mentally impaired teenager; in his presence, the mother frequently made disparaging remarks regarding his intelligence level and his capacities.

I have come across members of the clergy who have struggled because of the behavior of their teenage children. They wrestle with whether they should stay in ministry in light of the admonition in 1 Timothy 3:5 (NIV): "If anyone does not know how to manage his own family, how can he take care of God's church?" Given that in the first century a sixteen-year-old would have been considered an adult and likely married, this text should most likely be taken as referring to children rather than teenagers with mental health issues. On the other hand, it is true that there can be times when mental health issues in a family can create some tension between a pastor's responsibility to his family and his responsibility to his church ministry.

Sometimes families may not be aware that a family member has a mental health issue until it manifests itself in some unhealthy manner, such as, depression, anxiety, paranoia, drug use, or attempted suicide. Some parents have devoted years of effort to raising a child to adulthood without fully realizing that he or she had a handicap. The realization has only come slowly through information accumulated through the school system, doctors, and other sources.

In this short chapter, I do not propose to elaborate on the various mental health issues people face.

Rather, I want to share a few insights that come out of my own family's experiences and that may help all of us move forward in faith and hope.

1. The Church Needs to Talk Openly about Mental Health Issues

Mental health seemed to have been a taboo subject in many of the evangelical churches that I grew up in. In fact, it was rarely addressed. One got the impression that people either felt helpless or fearful of the subject and therefore wouldn't talk about it. This must change. Researchers are now telling us that one in four adults has experienced or will experience some form of transient or permanent mental health issue.[36] This means that mental health issues are far more common than we care to acknowledge. Amy Simpson's book *Troubled Minds: Mental illness and the church's mission* has helped me to think through some of the issues in this chapter. She stated:

> In many churches, intentionally or unintentionally, the over-riding emphasis is on "victorious living," with the basic assumption that real Christians don't have problems—or at least not crippling, persistent problems that a prayer or two won't cure. Some churches purposely embrace this as a basic doctrine...This is in complete contradiction to what Jesus said: "Here on earth you will have many trials and sorrows. But take heart, because I have overcome the world" (John 16:33).[37]

The first time I realized the lack of mental health publications with a spiritual perspective, as well as other resources in the church community, was the summer my wife had a basal skull fracture. Following her accident, she suffered from depression and severe headaches, and full cognitive healing took three years.

I soon discovered that my wife was not alone in suffering from such problems. While pastoring in two churches, I discovered that there were many mental health issues in those congregations, almost all of which were kept confidential. I can remember privately addressing a broad range of mental health issues and referring people to mental health professionals. The issues included depression, cutting, bipolar disorder, anxiety disorder, personality disorder, and many other issues listed in the Diagnostic and Statistical Manual of Mental Disorders. I also learned that people I knew of from other churches (in two cases a pastor and in another case a board member) had committed suicide. That gave me further cause to think about what kind of church resources exist for families which have a member with a mental health disorder.

Families can feel guilty for being slow to realize that a mental health issue was more serious than they thought, leaving them wishing they had done more to intervene. Parents can feel like failures when dealing with troubled teenagers; they may even succumb to irrational thoughts such as wondering why "God isn't favoring our family." People with mental health issues in our society are stigmatized and often shunned, and those practices get imported into the church. As a result, church families struggling with such issues may feel ashamed and compelled to be secretive about the matter. However, we should remember the words of Paul in 1 Corinthians 12:24-26 (NASB):

> God has so composed the body, giving more abundant honor to that member which lacked, so that there may be no division in the body, but that the members may have the same care for one another. And if one member suffers, all the members suffer with it; if one

member is honored, all the members rejoice with it.

2. The Church Needs to Offer Better Support to Those with Mental Health Issues

Churches also need to be more proactive in educating and equipping members of their congregations to understand mental health issues and provide support to those in need. There should be more sermons dealing with the challenging spiritual questions mental health issues give rise to. As Christians, we need to be people who love other people (in practical terms), accept other people as they are (without fear), and model grace (by showing patience, among other virtues). We should not be afraid to pray with people who are struggling. We should recognize that people being friendly with other people is one of the ways in which God loves them.

Wouldn't it be something if our churches created groups where people could share some of their challenges? I see divorce care, grief care, and addictions groups popping up in churches, but a support group for families dealing with mental health issues seems to still be some distance away. Can our churches be places where individuals with mental health issues can find encouragement, a listening ear, and hope?

3. Christian Families with Mental Health Issues Should Seek Help

Through my experience in my own family, I learned that I had to adjust my expectations to match the reality that I was facing. I had to learn how to effectively help people who were struggling with mental health issues to be able to cope. Prayer helps, but, short of a miracle, I had to change my thinking about the likelihood of a quick and easy recovery. It does no good to just wish things were different. Unless there is a miraculous deliverance, people need grace to face the reality in front of them.

It is also important for families with a member struggling with mental health issues to learn about the resources available in their community. These include medical, psychiatric, psychological, and spiritual resources and support groups of people who are struggling with similar issues. Families should make it a priority to access whatever resources in their community they can find that could be of help to their afflicted family member.

Families in this situation should also be prepared for the possibility that their advocacy for their family member will be misunderstood even though they know it is still necessary. They should also be prepared for the possibility that their family member's behavior will be misunderstood—every church has people in it who will not be equipped to understand mental health issues. Families should also be sure to establish healthy boundaries with their family member and not let other unhealthy people interfere with their commitment to doing the right things; families trying to help a troubled family member should make sure that they themselves stay safe and healthy.

Church boards and congregations should be reassured that pastors can be good pastors even though they have a family member with mental health issues. It doesn't mean that the gospel they preach is any less true or effective.

4. Churches Should Be Healing Communities

Churches, as well as struggling families, should inform themselves about some of the positive effects a worshipping faith community can have on a person with a mental health problem. A helpful resource in this regard is Harold Koenig's *Faith and Mental*

Health: Religious Resources for Healing.[38] This chapter is not primarily about sending people with mental health problems to professionals, but about the people of God being the people of God. When that happens, qualitative changes can take place. When that happens, churches will become places of encouragement, caring, and giving, communities which will speak for those who can't speak for themselves. Certainly, this will require churches to develop helping strategies and to learn how to access resources. But, more importantly, it will require churches to recover the ability to be healing communities and require Christians to be friends who will help to keep hope alive in those who desperately need hope. When the world sees how we show love to "the least of these," many more people may find the Good News spoken by Jesus' followers to be more convincing (Matthew 25:40 NIV, John 13:35). Our future hope for the full expression of the healing accomplished by the cross needs to be understood as a shared hope, kept alive for the entire faith community. So, "let us consider how we may spur one another on toward love and good deeds, not giving up meeting together, as some are in the habit of doing, but encouraging one another" (Hebrews 10:24-25 NIV).

8
Hope Alive: Thanks for the Memories

"Just when the caterpillar thought it was over, it turned into a butterfly." – proverb

There were many parents in my generation (I am at the tail end of the Baby Boomers) who grew up in the church and then returned later, after they were married and had children, to raise their kids in the Christian faith. Their hopes were that their children would embrace the faith, remain in the church, stay out of trouble, and eventually marry someone who shared the same faith and worldview. Many of these parents had their hopes fulfilled as their children participated in the life of the church. However, many other good parents saw their children leave the church and the practice of the faith when they became youth and young adults.

I have witnessed some parents of grown children who exited the church become disillusioned with the church. Somehow they had been given the impression that if they faithfully raised their children in the church, then God owed them the result they wanted, almost as if they had earned points in God's loyalty program. They expected God to overrule their adult children's free will and keep them in the church. I have heard many Christian parents misquote Acts 16:31 (NIV): "Believe in the Lord Jesus, and you will be saved—you and your household." They take a promise that was given to an individual character in scripture and try to make the promise universal, again overriding the free will of their offspring. When we compare scripture with scripture, we realize that God gives every individual a free will and people must individually choose whether to place their faith in Him or not; He does not eclipse or usurp some people's free will, no matter how much we want Him to.

During my young adult years, I was a psychology undergraduate in university and was greatly influenced by behavioristic models of psychology on the subject of raising children. During the early years of raising our child, I remember believing that you could direct the life of a child by simply putting together the right ingredients—just like following a cake recipe—and get a precise outcome. So I ensured our child received all of the right ingredients—youth groups, church, community service, school study, sports, music lessons, family nights, and fun vacations to places such as Disneyland and the Grand Canyon. I have since grown in my thinking and theology to realize that we can give our children the best possible upbringing but once they reach adulthood they will be making choices for themselves that we don't get a vote on. Young adults who turn out badly don't necessarily do so as a result of bad parenting.

There are parents who give themselves too much credit—and other parents who load too much guilt on themselves unnecessarily. Many parents suffer quietly and deeply because their offspring have chosen not to walk with God. Their suffering is often deepened when they hear other parents in the church boast about what their children are doing, giving the impression that they should get the credit for it because they were "good parents." Of course, we should be pleased with our children's accomplishments. But we should also be aware of other parents' enormous struggle whose adult children have left home and checked out from being involved in the Christian faith community and from practicing the faith they were raised in. This kind of suffering (which can rightly be called grief) is experienced very privately and quietly. These parents can be tempted to feel guilty for the life choices and directions of their adult offspring. They can torture themselves with questions such as "If only we had been in another church when they were growing up" or "If only we had done this or that..."

When encountering such grieving parents, other people should be aware that when they ask personal questions regarding their nonbelieving family members, they are touching on sensitive, hurtful matters. Unless the information is offered, it is best for others not to ask for it and to just pray.

For the grieving parents themselves, the best response is to keep praying for their wayward children's well-being, to recognize that God has willed them into existence and that therefore the problem is God's problem. It is also helpful to remember that, as long as they are alive, God isn't finished with them. The last chapter in their lives has yet to be written. Perhaps at one time these wayward souls had evidenced a vibrant Christian faith, wanted to be baptized, and even served in the church. Perhaps, deep down, they sensed that there was something more to being a Christian than just being part of a Christian subculture.

In my family's case, our prayer for our family members who have drifted away from the faith is not that they will come back to the institution of the church—even though I value its potential for nurturing people in faith and drawing them into the faith community, being part of an institution is not enough. Our prayer is that they will come to a point that they will renew their faith in Christ and follow

Him on a vibrant faith journey. God calls us to put our hope, prayers, and faith in Him; we should accept that God is sovereign and place our confidence in Him alone. At some point, we must come to a place where— even if no one else around us continues to serve the only God who truly exists—we will still resolve to put our faith, hope, and trust in Him. Meanwhile, we live in the "now but not yet" and hold on with all our might to a God who is "able to do immeasurably more than all we ask or imagine" (Ephesians 3:20, NIV). We serve a living God who is almighty, and that keeps hope alive.

9

Hope Alive: My Earth Is Shaking

"I have told you these things, so that in me you may have peace. In this world you will have trouble. But take heart! I have overcome the world." – John 16:33 NIV

Where I live, near the coast of British Columbia, we have been told by the scientific community that our region is overdue for a megathrust earthquake. I have never had an experience of a natural disaster touching me personally. The closest I have come was a basement flooded with sewage, and that obviously doesn't qualify. But I have been living for the past decade in a part of the country which is continually being bombarded with ominous warnings about earthquake preparedness. I have also been struck by news reports of the suffering of others who have been devastated by natural disasters.

Manmade hazards and disasters, such as pollution, crime, terrorism, war, and power outages don't seem to raise a lot of ultimate questions for most people. We generally understand the suffering associated with these hazards as being linked to human negligence and even human evil. Where we can find ourselves asking deeper questions is when suffering happens due to natural disasters such as tsunamis, floods, earthquakes, wildfires, famines, landslides, avalanches, and tornados. When we see the monumental levels of death and suffering that a natural disaster can bring on a community, we often don't feel satisfied with saying, "The reason for this happening is a mystery." If you are like me, you may find yourself asking some variation of the question, "If God is all-good and all-powerful, why are so many innocent people suffering?" There is no answer to this question. We are not given an explanation for the mystery we are living in. God has not chosen to give us an explanation for the events that bring this kind of evil to the lives of people. But, at the same time, we are encouraged to believe that God is intimately involved with His creation and He has not withdrawn from what He has made.

I have wondered if natural disasters were a part of the created order, to which fallen humanity is now exposed, having been expelled from the Garden of Eden. Or is it that the fall has also impacted the created order, introducing natural disasters to a world that had previously been free of them? I believe it is both. The curse upon Adam extended to man's habitation as well. Consider Romans 8:21-23 (NIV):

> The creation itself will be liberated from its bondage to decay and brought into the freedom and glory of the children of God. We know that the whole creation has been groaning as in the pains of childbirth right up to the present time. Not only so, but we ourselves, who have the firstfruits of the Spirit, groan inwardly as we wait eagerly for our adoption to sonship, the redemption of our bodies.

Some things in the created order have mysteriously changed since the fall, and one day those things will be renewed and brought back to their pristine condition that God intended at the beginning.

Meanwhile, it is obvious that God allows natural disasters and the suffering natural disasters bring is somehow part of a much bigger picture—although how this is remains a mystery. I don't like this conclusion, but it reinforces the understanding that we live in mystery. Psalm 115:3 (NIV) has sometimes troubled me: "Our God is in heaven; he does whatever pleases him." I recognize that what God might ultimately call good, I might not call good in the interim. (Had I been living before dinosaurs became extinct, I would most likely not have thought them good.) My tendency is to call good what maximizes my pleasure, comfort, and security and minimizes my pain. However, scripture depicts God as identifying good coming out of at least some painful events. The Father's outlook on the humiliation and suffering of Jesus Christ during His crucifixion is found in Isaiah 53:10 (NASB): "But the LORD was pleased to crush him." The crucifixion was something planned for the ransom of humanity. It is an example of God allowing suffering for redemptive purposes based on an eternal perspective.

Natural disasters are also associated with the difficult times we are living in, including our concern with environmental issues. Consider Ecclesiastes 9:12 (NIV): "Moreover, no one knows when their hour will come: As fish are caught in a cruel net, or birds are taken in a snare, so people are trapped by evil times that fall unexpectedly upon them." That suffering occurs in the lives of people due to a natural disaster doesn't mean that those people were deserving of that suffering or that God was judging them. Many good people, including Christians, have also lost their lives in natural disasters. Consider Luke 13:1-5 (NIV):

> Now there were some present at that time who told Jesus about the Galileans whose blood Pilate had mixed with their sacrifices. Jesus answered, "Do you think that these Galileans were worse sinners than all the other Galileans because they suffered this way? I tell you, no! But unless you repent, you too will all perish. Or those eighteen who died

when the tower in Siloam fell on them—do
you think they were more guilty than all the
others living in Jerusalem? I tell you, no! But
unless you repent, you too will all perish.
In fact, any response to human suffering other than
compassion and humanitarian action should be looked
at with disdain.

I have discovered some biblical texts that associate
a few natural disasters with spiritual conflict on a
grander scale (for example, Exodus 9:15, Joel 2:30-31,
Matthew 24:7). But applying such explanations to
current events seems a bit presumptuous or even
foolhardy. We can, however, look forward to the
promise (2 Peter 3:13) that one day redeemed
humanity will enjoy the peace of a new earth.
Revelation 21:4-5 (NASB) describes it like this:

"And [God] will wipe away every tear from
their eyes; and there will be no longer any
death; there will no longer be any mourning,
or crying, or pain; the first things passed
away." And He who sits on the throne said,
"Behold, I am making all things new." And He
said, "Write, for these words are faithful and
true."

10
Hope Alive: Hung up on a Tree

"No victory without suffering." – J.R.R. Tolkien

In my business travels, I frequently see people spending a lot of money gambling through the purchase of lotto tickets. It has occurred to me that it can be easy for Christians to slip into superstitious thinking and believe luck or chance causes the events that happen in their lives.

It is a very different thing to see the events of our lives as being under the control of our wise, loving, and all-powerful God. "Providence" is a word that refers to God's ability to foresee the future, as well as God's preservation and governance of His created order to achieve His purposes. The fact is that God nourishes, preserves, cares for, and maintains the world and everything in it through His power and His wisdom. God cares about and takes care of what He has made, even to the smallest bird (Matthew 10:29). David commented in Psalm 104:27-28 (NIV), "All creatures look to you to give them their food at the proper time. When you give it to them, they gather it up; when you open your hand, they are satisfied with good things." Jesus said that from the very beginning He and His Father have always been at work (John 5:17). Hebrews 1:3 notes that all things are sustained by His mighty command. This suggests that all events in this world are governed by God's undisclosed, ever-present activity. This can be both comforting and discomforting because many things in life are incomprehensible. God's providence deals not just with the cosmos, earth, and nature, but also especially with people; some call this special providence. For example, Christ taught that all the hairs of our heads are numbered (Matthew 10:30). Paul commented that "in him we live and move and have our being" (Acts 17:28 NIV).

A Lesson from a Rock

I found myself deeply thinking about God's providence in my life after an event during an early summer morning drive to work. At the time, I generally started work around 4:30-5:00 a.m. This event occurred during the month of July. Normally, I would have had my driver's window wide open during these warm summer mornings, but on the morning of this event, for some reason, I didn't. As I was heading south towards the Alex Fraser Bridge, a rock hit the middle of my driver's side window, slicing it almost halfway across the glass. At first, I thought it must have been a bullet; it sounded like a bullet when it hit, and it caused damage like a bullet might have. Judging from the location of the cut across the glass, had the window been open (as it generally would have been), it would likely have hit me in the face or the neck. I couldn't think of why I had kept my driver's window closed that warm morning, but it would be theologically consistent for me to say that if God exists and God knows all things, that means that God would have known ahead of time that this event would occur.

When we receive the unexpected provision of a blessing, we recognize that every good thing comes from God (James 1:17). For example, when they needed a sacrificial ram, Abraham said to his son Isaac, "God will provide" (Genesis 22:8 NASB).

Abraham was asserting that God foreknows future events and needs and that therefore we need to give our concerns about the unknown to God, who can make a way out of things we don't understand. Further, Abraham was asserting, not just that God foreknows the future, but also that we can be confident in God's provision because God is working in the events of our lives. Providence is the reason we pray, "Give us this day our daily bread" (Matthew 6:11 NASB). Psalm 75:6-7 (NASB) tells us that promotion and demotion come from God, who "puts down one and exalts another." 1 Corinthians 4:7 informs us that our gifts and talents come from the Lord.

Most often what bothers us about providence can be put into this question: If God is so active in the world, then why does He allow people to do evil things?

However, I want to focus this discussion about God's providence on His children, believers. Jeremiah commented, "I know O LORD that a man's way is not in himself, nor is it in a man who walks to direct his steps" (Jeremiah 10:23 NASB). Proverbs 20:23 (NASB) says, "Man's steps are ordained by the LORD." I often remember my grandfather recalling the journey of his long life and commenting, "So many things in my life seemed to be almost given to me." He was using the language of providence, giving tacit acknowledgment of the fact that there is a Higher Power who gives good things to all human beings. Proverbs 16:9 (The Message) reassures believers with these words: "We plan the way we want to live, but only God makes us able to live it."

A Providential Tree

I want to tell you a true story about some tree planters who years ago were planting trees on the boulevard along Hastings Street in Vancouver. Most likely, they believed that they were planting trees to beautify the city. But I believe that one particular tree was planted to protect people from harm—including me and the customers in a Chinese restaurant named The Pelican. That might sound crazy, but let me explain.

It was a Wednesday morning several summers ago. I was parking a large truck (a five-ton vehicle with a 15,000-pound freezer box, built almost like a tank) before making a sales call on one of my accounts. I went into the building, logged the sales order into my software, and came out of the building—only to discover that the truck was gone. At first, I thought it had been stolen. And then I looked across the street. There was the truck, hung up on top of a thirty-year-old tree on the boulevard; the downed tree had restrained the truck from going any further. Apparently, the truck's air brakes had not held, and it had slowly rolled across five lanes of traffic during rush hour without hitting, hurting, or killing anybody. The traffic included a bus full of passengers whose path was now blocked by the truck. I stood there as if I'd been struck by lightning. I was experiencing so much inner turmoil, going over in my imagination all of the possible scenarios that could have happened. For the next three days, I had great difficulty sleeping as I replayed over and over how my life could have been seriously altered had someone been hurt or killed.

Then, three days later, while I was doing my devotions on my sun deck very early on Saturday morning, I found some consolation. The summer sun was slowly coming up, I could hear the birds singing, and the air was morning fresh. I was sipping a homemade Starbucks coffee while reading and reflecting on a passage in John Calvin's writings on God's providential care. It was a centering moment. I sensed the immediate presence of the Holy Spirit. I wept, and the heaviness I had been feeling lifted. I did what scripture tells us to do when our minds are burdened down with heaviness: "Cast all your anxiety on him for he cares for you" (1 Peter 5:7 NIV). I also pondered how the tree that my truck had hit could have had such a purpose in being planted that was unknown to anyone except God. I was convinced that God had arranged to have that tree planted there so that the people in the restaurant about thirty feet beyond the tree could safely enjoy their dim sum without a five-ton truck slamming into them. You may have difficulty with my conclusion, but it is a logical conclusion based on the clear teaching in scripture that God is active in His creation and there is no such thing as luck or chance.

Comfort in God's Providential Action

Nothing happens without God knowing it. Nothing takes place that the Lord has not already foreseen. Job 14:5 (NIV) says that "A person's days are determined; you have decreed the number of his months and have set limits he cannot exceed." Psalm 139:16 also states that our days are numbered. Behind all that happens in our lives in this world is the secret stirring of God's hand and His engagement in sustaining creation.

Like Job, what we often want from God is for God to give us an explanation of His secret activities and judgments regarding injustices, tragedies, and natural disasters. But we don't get such explanations. All we get is assurances that, even though things may seem confusing, wrong, and mixed up, God is directing things towards a right end and God will have the last word. Romans 11:33-34 (NASB) states, "Oh, the depth of the riches both of the wisdom and knowledge of God! How unsearchable are His judgments, and unfathomable His ways! For who has known the mind of the Lord, or who became His counselor?"

Deuteronomy 29:29 (NASB) affirms, "The secret things belong to the LORD our God, but the things revealed belong to us and to our children forever, that we may observe all the words of this law." In his suffering, Job found himself realizing that human wisdom comprehends only a tiny fragment of reality (Job 26:14, 28:21). Therefore, he concluded, "The fear of the Lord, that is wisdom" (Job 28:28 NASB).

It is right that we recognize God as the all-knowing Supreme Authority. So, what is the practical implication to acknowledging this? We must realize that though God acts providentially, we still have a responsibility to obey Him in what He has revealed to us. God's providence does not excuse us from living wisely (working, planning, investing, reaching out, praying). Proverbs 16:9 (NASB) says, "The mind of man plans his way, but the LORD directs his steps." This does not mean that we are free to neglect the stewardship of our lives or escape the responsibility for managing our lives to fulfill God's purposes. Rather, the fact of God's providence should help us to be peaceful in heart. Knowing that our plans, efforts, and abilities are in God's hand, we can rest assured that He will guide, bend, or constrain them as suits His purposes. Psalm 91:1 (NIV) says, "Whoever dwells in the shelter of the Most High will rest in the shadow of the Almighty," and Isaiah 49:25 (NIV) promises, "I will contend with those who contend with you."

It may sound strange, but if we can settle in our minds the certainty that God does act providentially, it can help us deal with our hardships. Let's briefly consider Joseph's story. If Joseph had focused on his brothers' bad treatment of him, he would never have been able to get over the hardship he had experienced. Instead, he turned his thoughts to the Lord and that allowed him to get over the injustice of being sold into slavery by his brothers. In Genesis 45:7-8 (NASB),

Joseph said, "God sent me before you ...to keep you alive... it was not you who sent me here, but God."

And let's consider Job's story. If Job had focused his attention on the Chaldeans, who had robbed him, he might have focused on revenge. But he recognized the disasters that had befallen him as something the Lord had permitted. He comforted himself with these words: "The LORD gave, and the LORD has taken away; blessed be the name of the LORD" (Job 1:21 NASB).

In summary, when we are unjustly wounded by people, if we can keep our thoughts centered on God's providence, we can gain peace from the insight that nothing happens to us that God hasn't permitted. It is likely that for some people life may feel unbearable because they have no certainty that God is acting providentially in their lives. Certainty about God's providence can set their spirits free from anxiety and fear. The psalmist affirmed a confidence in God's providential acts: "The LORD is for me" (Psalm 118:6 NASB); "In God I have put my trust; I shall not be afraid. What can mere man do to me?" (Psalm 56:4 NASB)

The Prayer of Heman

David concluded in Psalm 31:15 that his times were in God's hand. No matter how unstable and changing his life was, he was confident that his life was being governed by God. But you may be thinking, "I find it difficult to believe in God's providential working in my life because God seems so silent." This was the struggle of the writer of Psalm 88. The majority of us might be willing to say that we could put up with some hardship if our story ended like a Disney book with the words, "And they lived happily ever after"—in this life." But scripture is realistic that in this life, during our whole lifetime, hardship and difficulty may continue to the closing chapters of our life.

I want to explore this thought as it is reflected in Psalm 88 (NIV). This is a depressive prayer song, a lament, from an individual who experienced no "happily ever after" in this life. Something was missing for the author, and that something was hearing from God. In most of our Bibles, the preface to Psalm 88 says, "A song. A psalm of the Sons of Korah. For the director of music. According to *mahalath leannoth*. A *maskil* of Heman the Ezrahite." Heman is identified in 1 Kings. 4:31 as a very wise man. Heman is also identified in 1 Chronicles 6:33; 15:16-19 as one of the leading musically gifted Levites who ministered in worship during the time of David. It would be accurate to identify him as a leading priest or minister, a counselor, and a worship leader in his time. He was a man of God.

I want to look at some of the insights found in this psalm because I believe it can give us a more sobering sense of God's sovereignty and providence in the face of the suffering and pain that we encounter in our lives. It can help us think bigger picture and longer term.

1. The psalm begins with an opening prayer for deliverance (verses 1-2).

In the first verse—"LORD, you are the God who saves me; day and night I cry out to you"—we discover that the Lord's servant has been regularly praying for God to help him out of trouble. In verse 2, he says, "May my prayer come before you; turn your ear to my cry." He is begging for God to please hear him. The word "cry" ("*rinnah*" in Hebrew) can also indicate a loud scream. Sometimes people have been seen to pray this way in a worship service, a prayer room, at the Wailing Wall in Jerusalem, at Urbana, or at some ecstatic conference. It is the language of weeping and bloodshot eyes. This servant of God freely expressed his frustrations to the Heavenly Father. This raises an interesting question: Do we feel free to express ourselves to the Father—or would we rather complain to human ears?

2. The psalm continues with Heman praying regarding his impending death (verses 3-8).

The psalm continues in verses 3-5, "I am overwhelmed with troubles and my life draws near to death. I am counted among those who go down to the pit; I am like one without strength. I am set apart with the dead, like the slain who lie in the grave, whom you remember no more, who are cut off from your care." What is going on here with Heman? We get a sense that he is alive but feels dead on the inside. He doesn't feel as if God is with him. He doesn't feel that God is there for him. In fact, he feels that God has rejected him: "You have put me in the lowest pit, in the darkest depths. Your wrath lies heavily on me; you have overwhelmed me with all your waves. You have taken from me my closest friends and have made me repulsive to them. I am confined and cannot escape" (verses 6-8).

3. The psalm then portrays God's delay in coming to the aid of Heman (verses 9-12).

A summary of the psalmist's feelings is as follows. He feels "without strength" (verse 4), as if he is already dead (verse 5), and as if he is in the "lowest pit" and the "darkest depths" (that is, he feels depressed, verse 6). He feels the pressure of God's perceived displeasure, and he feels the loss of close friends, missing their fellowship and encouragement (verses 7-8). He feels "grief" (verse 9), and there is no relief.

One of Heman's most vexing problems is his belief that God has allowed this trouble to happen to him— a belief that fits with the idea that God acts sovereignly and providentially. But he goes further in accusing God directly: "You have put me...You have taken from me...and...made me..." (verses 6 and 8). Saying that God has allowed something is quite different from saying God has caused something. But Heman is hurt, and he believes that God has afflicted him and oppressed him unjustly. He does not understand. His question is our question: "Why me. Lord?" We need to be cautious about attributing to God the cause of our suffering. We also need to be cautious about basing our beliefs about God on difficult life experiences.

In verse 9, Heman returns to what he said in verse 1: "I call to you every day." A definite issue here is the perceived silence of God, and this leads Heman to wrestle with the Lord in prayer: "Do you show your wonders to the dead? Do their spirits rise up and praise you? Is your love declared in the grave, your faithfulness in Destruction? Are your wonders known in the place of darkness, or your righteous deeds in the land of oblivion?" (verses 10-12). Heman seems to be interrogating God, putting God on trial. There is a sense that this minister is saying to God, "I want to be able to tell others how marvelous You are, but I have been suffering and suffering, and You are not answering my prayers." Tim Keller notes that times of darkness reveal whether we got into a relationship with God in order for God to serve us, rather than in order for us to serve him.[39] Darkness reveals our motives! It's not surprising that this was the basis of Satan's accusation against Job: "Does Job fear God for nothing?" (Job 1:9 NIV)

4. Heman is desperate as he senses no deliverance from the Lord (verses 13-18).

In verse 13, Heman repeats, "But I cry to you for help, LORD; in the morning my prayer comes before you." God is the first thought on his mind for the day. God is his priority. This is a godly man who has been taught that the Lord hears the prayers of His people. His faith question is: "Why have You allowed me to experience this kind of misery and sadness?" When we have experienced God's goodness and experienced closeness and union with Him—in our devotional times, our service, and our worship—then the experience of extended suffering can be deeply depressing. Heman complains, "Why, LORD, do you reject me and hide your face from me?" (verse 14) The issue here seems to be that Heman doesn't feel that God loves him.

In verse 15, Heman continues, "From my youth I have suffered and been close to death; I have borne your terrors and am in despair." This worship minister mentioned earlier in verse 3, "My life draws near to death." It's unclear whether this believer has been suffering all his life, or if he is just angry with God and saying, "God, You have never cared about me my whole life." We sometimes say such things in our anger—and God can handle it!

Heman continues in verses 16-18: "Your wrath has swept over me; your terrors have destroyed me. All day long they surround me like a flood; they have completely engulfed me. You have taken from me friend and neighbor—darkness is my closest friend." Tim Keller has made the observation that spiritual darkness can last a long time. You can do all the right things, pray, and yet have everything go wrong for extended periods. After all, Jesus met a bad end, and we are not above Jesus.[40] The truth is that we can go all our lives and not know what God's purpose was for something that we have suffered physically, mentally, emotionally, and spiritually. This psalm ends on a sour, downbeat note—there is no closure to Heman's suffering.

Some Concluding Thoughts on Psalm 88

This psalm of lament does not end with any overt statement of hope. It ends with Heman's questions seemingly unresolved. So why is this psalm in the Bible? This psalm raises a good question: Does a providential God really care about how I feel? Does He hear my aching prayers? Does God really care about our suffering experiences? Where do we find comfort in a psalm such as this?

One point is obvious. The fact that God had this suffering worshipper's prayer included in the inspired Word of God is an eternal statement that God does understand. God has not stopped being God. God was providentially active in Heman's life. Heman was used in the faith community as a wise counselor, worship leader, musician in the house of God, priest, and man of prayer. Maybe Heman thought he'd be remembered for being a good musician, songwriter, or preacher...but God has him remembered as one whom God hears in a fallen, broken, sin-affected world. He is an example for us in that God heard every prayer that Heman uttered. God had a providential purpose for the very words of this servant's prayer. This psalm stands as evidence and a witness to every generation of believers that God is listening, near to us, and providentially at work—even though there is a mystery to His providential activities. Therefore, we should give thanks that God wants to help us in our suffering and sometimes that may come by guiding us to change our expectations. There are harsh realities we must face in this life. The cross was about harsh reality! In spite of this, God calls us to trust in His providential care. He calls us to grow and discover grace where we experience darkness, to be able to say with Job—if we have to—that "though he slay me, yet will I hope in him" (Job 13:15 NIV).

In this regard, I am often encouraged by several texts of scripture that are functionally prayers:

> Yours, LORD, is the greatness and the power and the glory and the majesty and the splendor, for everything in heaven and earth is yours. Yours, LORD, is the kingdom; you are exalted as head over all. Wealth and honor come from you; you are the ruler of all things. In your hands are strength and power to exalt and give strength to all. (1 Chronicles 29:11-12 NIV)

> [Your] dominion is an eternal dominion; [your] kingdom endures from generation to generation...[You] do as [you] please with the powers of heaven and the peoples of the earth. No one can hold back [your] hand or say to [you]: "What have you done?" (Daniel 4:34-35 NIV)

> Our Father in heaven, hallowed be your name, your kingdom come, your will be done on earth as it is in heaven. Give us today our daily bread. And forgive us our debts, as we also have forgiven our debtors. And lead us not into temptation, but deliver us from the evil one. (Matthew 6:9-13 NIV)

11
Hope Alive: The Mystery of Misery

"Everybody who tells you how to act has whiskey on their breath." – John Updike, Rabbit, Run

With all the books on the market, why publish another book that deals with the problem of pain? During my years in graduate school studying philosophy, it occurred to me that the academic discipline that battles the most against theism (belief in the existence of God) is philosophy. It was interesting to discover that there were a number of philosophers who had argued against theism as a result of painful life experiences or "the problem of evil." Examples include Charles Darwin after the death of his daughter[41] and J.J.C. Smart.[42] Inability to reconcile the existence of God with the problem of evil/pain fueled their construction of an atheistic philosophical position.

But I don't need to read the lives of philosophers to know that people construct their outlook on life based on the experiences they have lived through. In my 55 plus years of life, I have felt this tendency in myself and also seen it in the lives of others. A person is dumped by a spouse and becomes very bitter regarding the life of faith—where was God? Other people have endured years of vocational disruption, and it has jaded their outlook and sidetracked their faith journey—where was God? I could cite multiple examples of people who have struggled to believe in

God in the face of terminal cancer, betrayal, unemployment, addiction, poverty, failure, and depression. In this book, I have shared some painful experiences in my family's journey, revealing both the mess and the hope that we discovered while going through difficult times. My purpose has not been to sugarcoat or over-spiritualize the hardships, but to talk about the grace and hope we discovered while walking through the maze. God gives grace when we need it, where we need it, and we have discovered that when we persevere through difficulty, hope grows.

Some Words from Peter

I have found myself being intrigued by the aged apostle Peter's comments on suffering, which he addressed to the faith community in 1 Peter 4:12-19 (NIV):

> Dear friends, do not be surprised at the fiery ordeal that has come on you to test you, as though something strange were happening to you. But rejoice inasmuch as you participate in the sufferings of Christ, so that you may be overjoyed when his glory is revealed. If you are insulted because of the name of Christ, you are blessed, for the Spirit of glory and of God rests on you. If you suffer, it should not be as a murderer or thief or any other kind of criminal, or even as a meddler. However, if you suffer as a Christian, do not be ashamed, but praise God that you bear that name. For it is time for judgment to begin with God's household; and if it begins with us, what will the outcome be for those who do not obey the gospel of God? And, "If it is hard for the righteous to be saved, what will become of the ungodly and the sinner?" So then, those who

suffer according to God's will should commit themselves to their faithful Creator and continue to do good.

When people encounter extreme or prolonged events that bring suffering, it is instinctive to question why. Why me? Why my family? I remember one woman saying to me, "I have been trying to figure out the whip on my life for years." These are familiar questions to people who have reflected on the reason for the suffering they experience. We know that no one is immune to suffering and difficulty. Job 5:7 (NIV) says, "Man is born to trouble as surely as sparks fly upward." Whether arising from want, need, sadness, unfair treatment, unpopularity, loneliness, or various health issues, suffering can be distressing. There can be days and times when God seems unfair and it seems that there is no possible help or answer.

Yet, if we realize that God loves this world—that God loves us—then does that not mean that God grieves over human suffering? The Bible tells us that Jesus wept over the suffering the people in Jerusalem would face.

Peter wrote the book of 1 Peter to the dispersed churches located in the northern Roman provinces of Asia Minor, an area which Paul did not visit and which may have been evangelized by Peter between the Council of Jerusalem in AD 48 and the beginning of Emperor Nero's persecution of Christians in Rome in AD 64. Around AD 64, the situation of Christians in the Roman Empire was very uncertain. Persecution had already begun in Rome, and Peter was writing to the Christians in Asia Minor to address the various kinds of suffering Christians were facing (1:6f, 3:13-17; 4:12-19; 5:9). There were trials (1:6), there was unjust suffering (3:13-22), there was persecution (4:12-19), and there was suffering for doing good, the undeserved suffering of Christians linked with the will of God. But Peter was not writing primarily to warn Christians about the coming suffering. He was writing to talk about how Christians should behave when undergoing suffering (4:12-5:11). Above all, Peter wanted to convey a message of hope to Christians facing suffering.

Some Words from Paul

Many theologians believe that 1 Peter bears traces of the influence of some of Paul's writings. We do know that Paul was certainly one who could write at length on the subject of Christian suffering. Consider Paul's words in 2 Corinthians 12:7-10 (NASB):

> There was given me a thorn in my flesh, a messenger of Satan to torment me...I implored the Lord three times that it might leave me. And He said to me, "My grace is sufficient for you, for power is perfected in weakness." Most gladly, therefore, I will rather boast about my weaknesses, so that the power of Christ may dwell in me. Therefore I am well content with weaknesses, with insults, with distresses, with persecutions, with difficulties, for Christ's sake; for when I am weak, then I am strong.

Paul also wrote to another group who were suffering in Philippians 1:27-30. The church at Philippi in northern Greece was the first church that Paul founded in Europe, around AD 50.[43] Now, about AD 61-63, his colleague Epaphroditus[44] had reported to Paul that his friends in Philippi were facing a double problem—there was conflict among them and they were experiencing strong hostility from the pagan society around them. Paul wrote to this suffering church from a Roman prison, encouraging the members to live in unity and show courage. Here are his words from Philippians 1:27-28 (NIV):

> Whatever happens, conduct yourselves in a manner worthy of the gospel of Christ. Then, whether I come and see you or only hear about you in my absence, I will know that you stand firm in the one Spirit, striving together as one for the faith of the gospel without being frightened in any way by those who oppose you. This is a sign to them that they will be destroyed, but that you will be saved—and that by God.

Clearly the members of this faith community were frightened by the persecution and suffering they were experiencing. The word "frightened" that Paul used is used in Greek literature to refer to the uncontrollable stampede of horses that have been startled or spooked. We don't know exactly what brought about this fear in the Philippian Christians, but in verse 30 Paul compared the conflicts he experienced during his first visit to Philippi (Acts 16:6-40) with the disturbances presently going on. We can guess that the opposition was from those who embraced other worldviews and were hostile to the Christian gospel.

Because Philippi was a Roman military colony, it was especially devoted to the emperor. The cult of the emperor included giving him the divine titles of "lord" and "savior." At every public event, the people would proclaim "Caesar is lord" in the same way that we sing the national anthem at public events. The problem for Christian believers was that they were devoted to another Lord and this aroused suspicion and hostility from their neighbors. A Christian simply could not proclaim that Caesar is lord. To top it off, Christians' lord (Christ) had been crucified by a Roman lord, thus branding Jesus forever as an enemy of the state.

What the Christians of first-century Philippi couldn't see is that by AD 480 Christianity would dominate Philippi and that by the sixth century most of those living in Philippi would belong to the Christian church![45] The Philippian Christians living a life worthy of the gospel in the first century would sow the seeds of that future. But it would require living a life governed by faith and not fear.

Paul went on to say in Philippians 1:29 (NIV):
For it has been granted to you on behalf of Christ not only to believe in him, but also to suffer for him.

Paul's letter to the Philippian church has a lot to say about the problem of suffering. It addresses questions such as, "How can God be good and all-powerful and yet create a world in which suffering is often very intense?" Paul was suffering when he wrote this letter. He had done nothing worthy of blame, yet he was awaiting a trial that could result in him being executed as a criminal (Philippians 1:13-14,17,20). The Philippian Christians were also suffering at the hands of hostile unbelievers from their own society (Philippians 1:28).

Perhaps the question for the Philippian church was: "Why does an all-powerful and all-merciful God allow His people to be exposed to abuse from civic authorities and to the violence and evil in the world?" Twenty-first-century Syrian and Iraqi Christians could ask the same question. We can conjecture that maybe the church at Philippi was struggling with such questions to the point of doubting God's power or goodness. Many Christians conclude that because they are suffering God must be angry with them or withholding blessing from them. It is possible that there were a few in the Philippian church who were trying to convince people that there was no place for suffering in Christian experience.

But Paul would have nothing to do with such false teaching. Instead, Paul's message was that he was filled with joy in the midst of a hard situation. Paul was not joyful because he thought people ought to laugh at pain or because he thought that suffering is good. But how could Paul be joyful in prison? How can we be joyful in the midst of internal and external stresses?

Many of us unthinkingly accept our culture's view of what joy is: Joy is health and wealth; joy is success; joy is a lack of pressure or hardship; joy is maximized pleasure and minimized pain. We are uncomfortable discussing joy in the midst of hardship. We just want the hardship to go away and allow us to enjoy smooth sailing through life. Yet the hardship would not go away for Paul or for the Philippian church. That is why Paul had to address the false idea that if you're really a Christian, you won't suffer. Suffering comes with being born, with being a Christian, and with being a Christian witness. Paul's understanding of suffering was based on Christ's teaching on discipleship—that servants are to be like their master. Because Christ suffered, we will too. Paul did not present simplistic answers to the question of suffering (there is mystery in this). But he knew that God often works through suffering and weakness to foster growth and to accomplish His goals.

This is why Paul said. "It has been granted." The Greek word for "granted" is *eucharisthe*, which means "gifted." Paul said that the believer is gifted with two things—faith and the ability to endure suffering. Who wants to be gifted with suffering? Many of us would like to ask, "Can I take a pass on this?" The answer is no. Whether we want it or not, the gift is needed. Christians are to live on behalf of (as an extension of) Christ, just as Christ lived and died on behalf of this broken world. That, in part, is an explanation of why salvation includes suffering. The path to eternal glory includes going through the suffering of the cross.

Paul was not being morbid. He was not celebrating suffering in itself. He was celebrating that God's purposes were being done in the midst of suffering. This is why he said that suffering has been granted to us "on behalf of Christ." It was no accident that the Philippians were suffering, nor was it a punishment from God. Suffering was not a sign that God was angry with them. It was a sign that His favor was resting on them, that they were children of God. The Philippians were called to believe in Christ (a gift of God)—and they were called to endure pain, suffering, and hardship for Christ (also a gift of God).

As odd as it may seem, we are told to be at peace with the idea that suffering for the sake of Christ is part of a Christian's calling. Paul wrote in 2 Timothy 3:12 (NIV), "Everyone who wants to live a godly life in Christ Jesus will be persecuted." It is good to remind ourselves that the New Testament presents suffering as God's means of achieving His gracious purposes, both in Jesus (Hebrews 2:10) and in all believers (James 1:3-4; 1 Peter 1:6-7). Jesus himself said in John 16:33 (NIV), "In this world you will have trouble. But take heart! I have overcome the world."

Paul concluded his encouragement to the Philippians with one more thought, in Philippians 1:30 (NIV):

You are going through the same struggle you saw I had, and now hear that I still have.

The Philippians knew about Paul being persecuted both in Philippi (Acts 16:16-40) and in Jerusalem (Acts 21:27-26:32). The Philippians were now facing the same kind of persecution. Paul shared his own current situation in a Roman prison to encourage the Philippian Christians as they faced hardships. His letter was intended to set their minds at rest—by stating that his suffering in prison chains was evidence that he was in Christ. Paul was overcoming his depressing situation by placing his confidence firmly in Christ, and he was encouraging the Philippian Christians to do likewise. For Paul, the Christian life involved conflict and spiritual warfare (Ephesians 6:12)—there is no such thing as a spiritually demilitarized zone. Spiritual darkness and mischief don't take Sundays or vacations off. But the war we fight is a war fought with God's assistance.

Theological Explanations for Suffering

I have said that many have fallen away from faith in God as a result of suffering pain and evil. But Peter and Paul are reminders that many other people have had their faith in God strengthened while going through suffering.

There are many ways people can suffer, but reflecting on this issue theologically can equip us to handle suffering and remind us that we still live in hope. I would like to briefly review some of the broad stroke explanations for suffering.

First, a theological explanation for suffering starts with the fact that God has created a creation that is also free. Capon comments that not only are humans free, but the entire fabric of creation (the animal kingdom, the natural order, and the cosmos) is also endowed with freedom, making the world a risky and dangerous place.[46] Capon puts it this way:

> The world…is not stage-managed by God…It is rather a place in which all things are free within the limits of the style of their own natures—and in which all things are determined by the way the natures of other things impinge upon them.[47]

Second, there is the reality of the disobedience and fall of Adam and Eve, which has impacted the human race and the created order. Genesis 3:16-19 notes that the environment has been impacted and pain in

93

childbearing has been increased. Genesis 2:17 indicates that death—and all the suffering that precedes it—has entered the world. Paul noted in Romans 8:19-22 that creation groans and awaits its liberation from bondage. Paul concluded in 1 Corinthians 15:26 (NASB) that death is our "last enemy." Yet the believer lives in the hope that one day the created order will be healed and God will make everything new. Redeemed humanity will live in that healing.

Third, because many kinds of suffering have been introduced into the created order by sin, then we must acknowledge that some of the suffering we encounter may be a consequence of sin. We can suffer because of immoral decisions (e.g., drunk driving, unethical lifestyles). Wrong choices can come back to haunt us. Intermittently, scripture depicts sinful and foolish people eclipsing God's desire for them to flourish and short-circuiting a longer life because of the reign of sin in their lives (Proverbs 2:21-22). Hebrews 12:6 notes that God in his mercy occasionally uses discipline to help keep the believer from straying away from Him. Paul commented that under such circumstances God might permit suffering to draw a person to repentance (1 Corinthians 5:1-8).

Fourth, because we live in communities and families, our social choices and interactions have an impact on others. We can suffer because of the choices of others, and others can suffer because of the choices we make. When we look at the Old and New Testaments, we can see whole groups, communities, and nations experiencing suffering because of their disregard for honoring God and obeying His commandments. Nineveh in Jonah's time would be an example, but we can also read about other nations that were singled out for judgment because of their hostile policies towards their neighbors, particularly toward the nation of Israel. It is intriguing that God also used the nations of Babylonia and Assyria to punish Israel and Judah for disobeying God. In the book of Judges, God used foreign nations to inflict suffering on Israel when Israel strayed from God. I probably don't have to make an extended case for the fact that the sin of an individual can have enormous consequences; we can simply explore the biblical examples of Achan, Demas, and Alexander the coppersmith (2 Timothy 4:14). A discussion of good leadership and poor leadership can also help us explore the subject. Paul spoke these words to those who oppressed the church from within: "Do not be deceived: God cannot be mocked. A man reaps what he sows" (Galatians 6:7 NIV). In our vernacular, we might say, "What goes around comes around." One of the conclusions we can draw from reading scripture is that one person's sins can have intergenerational consequences (see Exodus 34:7; 20:5). One of the most serious decisions we can make is to reject Christ's invitation to indwell us and transform our lives. For Israel, rejecting Christ led to experiencing God's judgment (Matthew 12:38-45).

Fifth, a less explored idea is that suffering may be a part of the process that God uses to purify our lives for service and keep us dependent on Him. Hebrews 12:7 (NIV) comments, "Endure hardship as discipline; God is treating you as his children." James pointed out that trials can bring us closer to a holy God (James 1:2-3). Hebrews 5:8 (NASB) tells us that Jesus "learned obedience from the things which He suffered." If we can keep our faith focus on the Lord during times of suffering, there can be things that we learn while going through the crucible. It's quite possible that some of the deeper lessons of life are learned only through suffering and difficulty. This is different from saying that God is the cause of the suffering or the source of pain for the purposes of teaching us a lesson;

that would make Him a sadistic God. We are left with the option of either trusting that God's redemptive purposes are being worked out or despairing. But let's be cautious about telling people they are suffering so they can learn a lesson. This can be patently false when directed towards people suffering from things such as terminal cancer and mental illness—it's bad theology!

Sixth, there is the possibility that God may be permitting suffering in order to speak through our lives and our testimony to comfort others. In John 9:3 (NIV), Jesus said that a particular blind man had been allowed to suffer in order that "the works of God might be displayed in him." God might work in your life through suffering to inspire others by your example of how to handle difficulty and suffering. Those who have been through various kinds of suffering often can be a source of effective comfort to others when they share how God has comforted and sustained them. Paul concluded,

> Praise be to the God and Father of our Lord Jesus Christ, the Father of compassion and the God of all comfort, who comforts us in all our troubles, so that we can comfort those in any trouble with the comfort we ourselves receive from God. (2 Corinthians 1:3-4 NIV)

Seventh, many of God's faithful followers may be experiencing suffering because of God's timetable and historical designs. I have often reflected on this in regards to some of the things innocent Christians (and others) have experienced in places such as Syria and Lebanon or in the historic destruction of cities such as Jerusalem, Rome, and Constantinople.

I want to emphasize that much of human suffering has no explanation other than in the mysterious purposes of God. It remains in the realm of mystery. This brings me back to Paul's experience of some physical handicap or weakness from which he had been given no relief and for which he had been given no explanation. Paul's conclusion was that his weakness was a constant reminder not to rely on his own human abilities (intellect, education, skills, ethnic privilege) but to recognize that the power at work in him was of God despite his weakness.

Certainly there are some cases where a believer suffers for no disclosed reason; this is the thesis of the book of Job. Job loved and worshiped God, and yet he suffered. His three comforters were convinced that Job could not be innocent. In the end, God never explained to Job the reason for his suffering (although the reader is made aware of dark spiritual mischief). Instead, what God did was to ask Job a series of questions to make the point that some things are beyond human comprehension. Job was invited to accept his suffering without questioning God's wisdom or justice.

Enduring suffering seems to be a question of attitude. We need to ask ourselves: In the face of suffering, what am I going to do in order to grow from it and further God's eternal purposes? Some of the saddest people can be those who wallow in self-pity and bitterness, all the while taking a sort of delight in blaming God for their suffering. Job's attitude is an inspiration: "Though He slay me, yet will I hope in him" (Job 13:15 NIV).

When we as individuals or as a church are experiencing suffering, it is reasonable for us to reflect on possible reasons why God may have allowed it. If we need to repent of some sin and rededicate our lives to Christ, then start there. If we have not been nurturing our lives with God's Word or praying for God to reveal the reasons for our suffering or difficulty, then start there. It's reasonable to pray and ask God: What are You trying to say to me? What are You trying to teach me? What steps should I take? Maybe there is no lesson to be learned in this suffering, just a mysterious call to trust and be at peace. If that is the case, we can pray to God to help us get there. If you are facing mysterious suffering, I encourage you not to be alone in this process but to be engaged in a faith community, as fellowship can provide you with the listening ears of caring friends. Peter concluded in 1 Peter 4:16,19 (NASB):

> But if anyone suffers as a Christian, he is not to be ashamed, but is to glorify God in this name...Therefore, those also who suffer according to the will of God shall entrust their souls to a faithful Creator in doing what is right.

In the midst of suffering, a good question to ask is: "If [God] does help...how on earth does he do it?...the ultimate act by which God runs and rescues creation is the Incarnation."[48] I personally draw encouragement from Jesus, who knew that the final word was not crucifixion (suffering) but resurrection (freedom, healing, and renewal). Regardless of the kind of suffering that may touch your life, I encourage you to resist getting stuck in self-pity or bitterness. Don't give up hope. Be at peace with the mystery. The psalmist asked himself, "Why, my soul, are you downcast? Why so disturbed within me? Put your hope in God." (Psalm 42:5 NIV) One day this, too, will pass, and the sight of Him will put everything into perspective!

Postscript

"One cannot imagine Saint Francis of Assisi talking about his rights." – Simon Weil

The chapters in this book were put together over a period of two months after I had experienced a severe ankle sprain. My wife reminded me that, prior to the sprain, I had commented that I could use some time off because of some writing projects I had in mind (this one included). I jokingly commented to my wife that my expressed wish for writing time off must have shot up to heaven like a prayer.

Perhaps my most difficult years are still ahead, as aging is filled with plenty of losses and there is yet the sting of death to face. So, I don't write as a soldier who can take off his armor yet. But, I carry on in faith and hope that the ultimate overcoming of pain and suffering was, is, and will be accomplished because of Calvary. Whether you've had the impression God is not answering your prayers for certain things to change, had a traumatic health issue, lost a job, experienced significant grief, been assaulted, been impacted by murder, struggled with family mental health issues, grieved over family members leaving the faith, or struggled with the issue of providence and the reality of natural disasters—all of which have been part of my journey—may your memory of who God is and His ultimate promises bring you hope. Jeremiah said, "Yet this I call to mind and therefore I have hope" (Lamentations 3:21 NIV). In illustrating that memory is the handmaid of hope, John Bunyan, author of *The Pilgrim's Progress*, wrote of Christian and Hopeful, two Christians who had been locked up in "Doubting

Castle." The name of the castle is symbolic of the spiritual state of these two people. It was memory and recall of biblical truth that helped set them free. Said Christian:

> What a fool...am I to lie in a stinking dungeon, when I may...walk at liberty? I have a key in my bosom, called promise that will...open any lock in "Doubting-Castle." Then Christian pulled it out...and...the door flew open with ease and...then he went to...the Iron Gate...the key did open it. Then they thrust open the gate to make their escape.[49]

It was in this way that Christian and Hopeful were set free.

One of the apostle Paul's prayers is that every Christian would "know what is the hope of His calling" (Ephesians 1:18 NASB). This hope is a certain, living hope. In fact, the Greek word here for hope (*elpis*) is a noun. We could speak of the late comedian Bob Hope in this way, "We have had a decade of Hope." Paul is saying that we can know the person and source of hope that keeps hope alive—Jesus. We are called to eagerly lean towards the plans that the Lord has for us to give us a hope and a future (Jeremiah 29:11). This is big picture thinking—to believe that no matter what the hardships, suffering, and mistreatment we face, the Lord will take us through to a guaranteed reservation in eternity. This is "the hope of His calling...the glory of His inheritance" (Ephesians 1:18 NASB). God has anchored our hope in heaven and the encouragement He gives us is to "hold fast the confession of our hope without wavering, for He who promised is faithful" (Hebrews 10:23 NASB). I conclude with a prayer for the reader: "Now may the God of hope fill you with all joy and peace in believing, so that you will abound in hope by the power of the Holy Spirit" (Romans 15:13 NASB).

Bibliography

Aquinas, Thomas. "The Cause of Evil," *An Introduction to Philosophy: Ideas in Conflict*, edited by Peter Windt. Saint Paul, Minnesota: West Publishing, 1982.

Brand, Paul, and Philip Yancey. "And God Created Pain," *Christianity Today*, vol. 38, no. 1 (January 10, 1994): 18-21.

Breese, Dave. *Seven Men Who Rule the World from the Grave.* Chicago, IL: Moody Press, 1990.

Bunyan, John. *The Pilgrim's Progress.* Westwood, NJ: Barbour and Company, Inc., 1985.

Capon, Robert Farrar. *The Third Peacock: The Problem of God and Evil.* Minneapolis MN: Winston Press, reprint 1986.

Carson, Herbert. *Facing Suffering.* Hertford, UK: Evangelical Press, 1978.

Dobson, James. *When God Doesn't Make Sense.* Wheaton, IL: Tyndale Press, 1993.

Geisler, Norman, and Ron Brooks. *When Skeptics Ask.* Wheaton, IL: Victor Books, 1989.

Hick, John. "The Problem of Evil," *An Introduction to Philosophy: Ideas in Conflict*, edited by Peter Windt. St. Paul, MN: West Publishing, 1982.

Israel, Martin. *The Pain that Heals.* New York: Crossroad Publishing, 1981.

Jobs, Steve. "Stanford commencement address June 12, 2005" in *The Stanford Report* (June 14, 2005). Retrieved from: http://news.stanford.edu/news/2005/june15/jobs-061505.html

Keller, Tim. "Heman's Cry of Darkness," *Real Spirituality—Prayer and Beyond* (November 4,

2007). Retrieved from: http://www.gospelinlife.com /heman-s-cry-of-darkness-5556

Koenig, Harold. *Faith and Mental Health: Religious Resources for Healing.* Templeton Press, 2005.

Kreeft, Peter. *Making Sense of Suffering.* Ann Arbor, MI: Servant Books, 1986.

Leibniz, Gottfried Wilhelm. "The Perfection of the World," *Introduction to Philosophy: Ideas in Conflict,* edited by Peter Windt. St. Paul, MN: West Publishing, 1982: 466-467.

Lehman Victor D. *The Pastor's Guide to Weddings & Funerals.* Valley Forge, PA: Judson Press, 2001.

Lewis, C.S. *A Grief Observed.* London: Harper Collins, 1961.

———. *The Problem of Pain.* London: Harper Collins, 1940.

———. *Till We Have Faces.* London: Harper Collins, 1956.

Moore, James. *The Darwin Legend.* Grand Rapids, MI: Baker Publishing, 1994.

Simundson, Daniel. *Where is God in My Suffering?* Minneapolis, MN: Augsburg Publishing, 1983.

Simpson, Amy. *Troubled Minds: Mental illness and the church's mission.* Downers Grove, IL: IVP Books, 2013.

Sire, James. *The Universe Next Door.* Downers Grove, IL: IVP, 1988.

Smart, J.J.C., and J.J. Haldane, *Atheism & Theism.* Oxford: Blackwell Publishers, 1996.

Stumpf, Samuel Enoch. *Socrates to Sartre.* New York: McGraw-Hill, 1993.

Taylor, Barbara Brown. *When God is Silent.* Lanham, MD: Rowman & Littlefield Publishers, 1998.

The Confessions of Augustine, translated by Rex Warner. Penguin Books, 1963.

Todd, Matthew. "A miracle with no metaphors," *Coquitlam Now,* vol. 12, no. 35 (Wednesday, August 30, 1995): 11.

_____. "Strap on a cap—it could save your life," *The Province* (Friday, September 1, 1995): A39.

_____. "A miracle on the fifth floor," *Advance* (January/February, 1996): 8-9.

Vanstone, W.H. *Love's Endeavor, Love's Expense: The Response of Being to the Love of God.* London: Darton, Longman and Todd Ltd., reprint 2015.

Verhoef, Edouard. "The church of Philippi in the first six centuries of our era," *HTS Teologiese Studies/ Theological Studies,* vol. 61, no. 1/2 (2005).

Wiersbe, Warren. *Why Us? When Bad things happen...* New Jersey: Power Books, 1984.

Wray, T.J. *Surviving the Death of a Sibling: Living through Grief when an Adult Brother or Sister Dies.* Potter/Ten Speed/Harmony, 2003.

Yancey, Phillip. *Where is God when it Hurts.* Zondervan, 1990.

Endnotes

INTRODUCTION

[1] C.S. Lewis, *The Problem of Pain* (London: Harper Collins, 1940) or *A Grief Observed* (London: Harper Collins, 1961); Peter Kreeft, *Making Sense out of suffering* (Ann Arbor, MI: Servant Books, 1986); Phillip Yancey, *Where is God when it Hurts* (Zondervan, 1990). The more academically inclined might want to seek out resources published by Josh McDowell, Norman Geisler, or J.J. Haldane.

[2] The English word "gospel" is derived from the Anglo-Saxon "godspell" ("good story"): "Biblical literature: Meaning of the term gospel," *Encyclopedia Britannica.* Retrieved from: http://www.britannica.com/topic/godspell Also see: Timothy Keller, *Preaching: Communicating Faith in an Age of Skepticism* (New York: Viking, 2015, p. 176): "The English word 'gospel' comes from the Middle English word 'Godspell' which derives from two Old English words: good and spell (story). In Old English 'to tell a story' was 'to cast a spell.'...The Gospel of Jesus Christ is the Good spell...It is the story that all other...stories point to."

CHAPTER 1

[3] Robert Farrar Capon, *The Third Peacock: The Problem of God and Evil* (Minneapolis, MN: Winston Press, reprint 1986), p. 64.

[4] There are a variety of published variations of this speech. One is "Steve Job's Stanford commencement address June 12, 2005" in *The Stanford Report* (June 14, 2005). Retrieved from: http://news.stanford.edu/news/2005/june15/jobs-061505.html

CHAPTER 2

[5] Matthew Todd, "A miracle with no metaphors," *Coquitlam Now*, vol. 12, no. 35 (Wednesday, August 30, 1995): 11. Matthew Todd, "Strap on a cap—it could save your life," *The Province* (Friday, September 1, 1995): A39. Matthew Todd, "A miracle on the fifth floor," *Advance* (January/February, 1996): 8-9.

[6] Paul Brand, "And God Created Pain," *Christianity Today*, vol. 38, no. 1 (January 10, 1994): 18-21.

[7] Capon, p. 3.

[8] Kreeft, p. 12.

[9] Kreeft, p. 15.

[10] Lewis, *The Problem of Pain*, p. 74.

[11] Lewis, *The Problem of Pain*, pp. 19-20.

[12] Lewis, *The Problem of Pain*, p, 17.

[13] Lewis, *The Problem of Pain*, pp. 19-20.

[14] *The Confessions of Augustine*, translated by Rex Warner (Penguin Books, 1963), pp. 150-151.

[15] John Hick, "The Problem of Evil," *An Introduction to Philosophy: Ideas in Conflict*, edited by Peter Windt (St. Paul, MN: West Publishing, 1982), p. 496.

[16] Samuel Enoch Stumpf, *Socrates to Sartre* (New York: McGraw-Hill, 1993), p. 244.

[17] Stumpf, p. 258.

[18] Lewis, *The Problem of Pain,* pp. 33-38.

[19] Kreeft, pp. 63-65.

[20] Stumpf, p. 271.

[21] Stumpf, p. 231.

[22] Dave Breese, *Seven Men Who Rule the World from the Grave* (Chicago, IL: Moody Press, 1990), p. 217.

[23] Lewis, *The Problem of Pain,* pp. 42-43.

[24] Warren Wiersbe, *Why Us? When bad things happen…* (New Jersey, Power Books, 1984), p. 21.

[25] Capon, p. 7.

[26] Norman Geisler and Ron Brooks, *When Skeptics Ask* (Wheaton, IL: Victor Books, 1989), p. 65.

[27] Wiersbe, p. 19.

[28] Gottfried Wilhelm Leibniz, "The Perfection of the World," *Introduction to Philosophy: Ideas in Conflict*, edited by Peter Windt (St. Paul, MN: West Publishing, 1982), pp. 466-467.

[29] Wiersbe, p. 51.

[30] James Dobson, *When God Doesn't Make Sense* (Wheaton, IL: Tyndale Press, 1993), pp. 34-41.

[31] Dobson, pp. 105, 218.

CHAPTER 3

[32] W.H. Vanstone, *Love's Endeavor, Love's Expense: The Response of Being to the Love of God* (London: Darton, Longman and Todd Ltd., reprint 2015), p. 9.

CHAPTER 5

[33] Barbara Brown Taylor, *When God is Silent* (Lanham, MD: Rowman & Littlefield Publishers, 1998), p. 70.

[34] T.J. Wray, *Surviving the Death of a Sibling: Living through Grief when an Adult Brother or Sister Dies* (Potter/Ten Speed/Harmony, 2003).

CHAPTER 6

[35] A resource for the prayers in this chapter is Victor D. Lehman's *The Pastor's Guide to Weddings & Funerals* (Valley Forge, PA: Judson Press, 2001), pp. 139, 141, 161-163.

CHAPTER 7

[36] *Leadership Journal*, 2010. "In this particular study 98% of clergy admitted to have seen some type of mental illness in their congregation but only 12.5% of these leaders felt it was being discussed openly and in a healthy way." Amy Simpson, *Troubled Minds: Mental illness and the church's mission* (Downers Grove, IL: IVP Books, 2013), pp. 53-54.

[37] Simpson, p. 104.

[38] Templeton Press, 2005.

CHAPTER 10

[39] Tim Keller, "Heman's Cry of Darkness," *Real Spirituality—Prayer and Beyond* (November 4, 2007). Retrieved from: http://www.gospelinlife.com/heman-s-cry-of-darkness-5556

[40] Keller.

CHAPTER 11

[41] James Moore, *The Darwin Legend* (Grand Rapids, MI: 1994), pp. 38-39, 46, 52.

[42] J.J.C. Smart and J.J. Haldane, *Atheism & Theism* (Oxford: Blackwell Publishers, 1996), pp. 66-67, 183-187.

[43] Acts 16:12-40, on Paul's on second missionary journey.

[44] Epaphroditus was an assistant to Paul in his missionary work. The Philippian Christians had sent him to Rome to minister to Paul.

[45] Eduard Verhoef, "The church of Philippi in the first six centuries of our era," *HTS Teologiese Studies/Theological Studies*, vol. 61, no. 1/2 (2005).

[46] Capon, pp.15-16.

[47] Capon, pp. 27-28.

[48] Capon, pp. 61-62.

POSTSCRIPT

[49] John, Bunyan, *The Pilgrim's Progress* (Westwood, NJ: Barbour and Company, Inc., 1985), p. 134.

CPSIA information can be obtained at www.ICGtesting.com
Printed in the USA
LVOW11s1338060816

498816LV00003B/6/P

9 780995 198302